Ritual Excellence

BEST PRACTICES FOR LEADING AND PLANNING LITURGY

JAMES W. FARWELL

Seabury Books
NEW YORK

Scriptures and additional materials quoted are from the Good News Bible © 1994 published by the British and Foreign Bible Society. Good News Bible © American Bible Society 1966, 1971, 1976, 1992. Used with permission.

Church Publishing
19 East 34th Street
New York, NY 10016

Cover design by Joseph Piliero
Typeset by Nord Compo

Library of Congress Cataloging-in-Publication Data
A record of this book is available from the Library of Congress.

ISBN-13: 978-1-64065-562-1 (pbk.)
ISBN-13: 978-1-64065-563-8 (eBook)

Contents

Introduction

This book offers principles and best practices for the curation, planning, and leadership of liturgical rites in the Episcopal Church. The conduct of liturgy that sounds the gospel clearly, with both openness and purpose, joy and *gravitas*, formality and freedom, sensitivity to the local and resonance with the universal, is crucial to ministry leadership that is faithful and effective. I hope that it will introduce important matters to those preparing for ministry, but also that it might be a helpful refresher to experienced clergy and provide them a "re-set."

Over the course of a typical priest's ministry, the most sustained contact they have with the largest number of people they serve will be through their leadership of the liturgy on Sundays. The leadership of liturgy is not simply another activity added on to mission, evangelism, pastoral care, and the like. As the assembly is being reconciled with the God who made and redeems us, leading the liturgical assembly is the fundamental act of pastoral care.[1] It is missional in its core—the result of the mission of God in the world and the place from which that mission continues in the assembly's departure into the world. It is not simply equipping for evangelism: it is itself the good news of the reconciliation by God in Christ, embodied and performed by an assembly singing the song of salvation before God. While a post-Christendom winnowing has been taking

---

1. Elaine Ramshaw, *Ritual and Pastoral Care* (Philadelphia, Fortress Press, 1987), p. 2.

place throughout Christian churches since at least the early 1980s, the liturgical assembly's worship remains the central act of the Christian community. In worship, the community who testifies to the reconciliation of God in Christ enacts that very reconciliation, standing in communion with God by grace, offering praise and prayer, lament and celebration, thanksgiving and remembrance, intercession and adoration before the One who has reconciled them.

The book is written primarily for clergy but it is my hope that it will also be helpful to laypersons with significant responsibility for or in the liturgies of their communities. The heart of the book is guidance on the concrete particulars of the Sunday liturgy, but it is not simply a how-to manual. It is my hope that, in the course of dealing with particulars, while also telling a little history and opening up the theology of our liturgical forms, this book will also *model a way of thinking about* liturgy that is consistent with the nature of ritual itself. Liturgy, like all ritual (more on these terms below), follows a script—whether written down or not—but the liturgy is far more than the script. Liturgy is a performance.[2] For that reason, its leadership is not only a matter of doing or leading the right things in the right order at the right time—though it is *certainly* that—but doing them *artfully* as the living worship of the community. There will not be just one measure of liturgical "artfulness," as the cultural, racial, ethnic, and situational location of liturgical performance and the style and skills of particular leaders

---

2. This term can sometimes mislead those unfamiliar with ritual theory. It does not imply acting out something that is not real. It means, in this context, that the primary mode of ritual is enactment, and the enactment of something in complete accord with deepest reality.

all come to bear on the art of liturgical curacy and leadership. However, ritual as a cross-cultural phenomenon has certain characteristics that should shape the way the leadership of rites is done, no matter the context. Planners and leaders will wisely work *with the grain of rituality* and not *against* it. There is also a theology—in fact, a whole theological conversation among ideas and images—enacted in the ritual structures of a particular faith community, and the wise leader also works with the grain of theology. Thus, within and across the range of ways that particular communities will celebrate liturgical worship, there are certain principles of performance that live within the specific practices and techniques of leadership, whatever the cultural location. To these principles, as well, the present book attends.

An Overview

In the first chapter, I will offer a sketch of where the Episcopal Church currently stands in its liturgical practice and its process of considering newly emerging ritual resources. Specifically, I will situate our present moment in the larger context of a shift represented by the 1979 *Book of Common Prayer* that has turned out to be perhaps even more significant than the framers of that book anticipated. I will also consider the ritual resources we have now, how they are to be used (or where ambiguity attends their usage), how diversity is expanding in the Episcopal Church, and what particular areas of concern are driving liturgical change.

Next, I will offer some general principles for Christian liturgy undergirded by what I would loosely call laws or characteristics of ritualization. As I noted above, ritualization is itself cross-cultural, and presents itself as fundamental human activity through history. Thus I hope these principles are applicable even to the growing diversity in the Episcopal Church in culture, ethnicity, race, gender, and language. It is in the process of ritualization that the liturgical and sacramental theology of the Episcopal Church lives, as it is manifested in the 1979 prayer book and expanded by subsequent liturgical resources.

The third chapter of the book will walk through the main resources that the Episcopal Church offers for the liturgy of the Lord's Day, element by element. These are, of course, the *Book of Common Prayer* 1979, supplemented by the *Book of Occasional Services* and *Enriching Our Worship*—the first volume of that series in particular. This is by far the longest chapter of the book. It is not exhaustive, but it does tend to the most significant elements of the liturgy for curation and planning, considering their theology and in some cases practical considerations and offering the occasional observation on church discussion of one form or another. The focus of the chapter is on the resources we curate.

In the fourth chapter I will give an overview of what seem to me the key factors that clergy bear in mind when curating liturgical forms and planning liturgies. This is rooted in my own years of experience as a parish priest as well as my work as a scholar. The focus of this chapter is the process of discernment involved in liturgical planning.

In the remaining chapters of the book, I walk through the rites most appropriate and most common to Sunday gatherings: Baptism and Eucharist. After a chapter dedicated to general principles and best practices, I turn to Eucharist and Baptism. I begin each with a brief theological account of the sacrament, and then turn to recommendations for practice. While every detail of practice that I outline may not apply to every single element of the liturgy in every context, my hope is that the practices I defend will provoke leaders who feel I have missed something important to their community to articulate or deepen their defense of their own practices. Note: I do not speak to every single moment or action of the liturgy, but to practices that are particularly important—or to practices that I see most commonly subject to mistakes or reflections of excellence, either in my students or in the many services I attend around the church.

At the end of the book are three appendices that I hope readers will find useful. The first offers a brief set of recommendations for more technical works on ritual theory. Readers with an interest in ritual theory, or who want to cultivate some knowledge in that area, may wish to pursue these resources. My recommendations about liturgy, rooted in my own study of ritual, will, I hope, be fairly accessible to the educated liturgical leader, but everything I say is underpinned by an interpretation of technical studies in ritual as well as liturgical theology. Most readers will be content with the principles and practices themselves, but for those who have the time and interest, the resources provided in Appendix A are well worth study.

In Appendices B and C, I offer the full text of two liturgical resources that the reader will want to have handy as I walk through the rites, especially in Chapters Three, Six, and Seven. These two are the expansive language versions of Rite II that have now been authorized for use, and the revision of

Rite II Prayer C that is also authorized for use. Meanwhile, the Episcopal Church's Standing Commission on Liturgy and Music is charged with developing a method to assess our learnings from these uses.

"Ritual Excellence"

A word about the title of this book is in order. The title certainly does not express or imply that the Christian community or its leaders aim for perfection or will achieve it. The Christian liturgical assembly is a broken assembly, part of a broken though beautiful creation, and the assembly will rarely embody fully in our lives what we enact in our assembly. Moreover, the Christian liturgical assembly is made up of humans for whom fallibility is an enduring feature of their nature. (Fallibility is not sin, but characteristic of the finitude and mortality of created existence.) As I have long told my students, with a phrase that I am sure I picked up in my own studies and whose origin is now lost to memory: in planning and leading liturgy, *we seek not perfection, but excellence.* Ritual excellence, as I conceive it, is to curate wisely, plan carefully, and lead with a simple elegance and solemn joy, all in ways that are consistent with what ritualization is and does. We seek such excellence because the matters that concern us in our worship through liturgy, composed of ritual practices, are nothing less than matters of death and life. Thus, liturgy deserves to be done with the best efforts we can muster, trusting that God's grace and mercy underwrites and empowers it at all. Ritual excellence is always our *aspiration* as curators, planners, and presiders.

Ecumenical Significance

A final note: I say that this book is aimed at liturgical leaders in the Episcopal Church. But given that liturgical revision and renewal in the last six decades has brought many of the major streams of Christian tradition closer together, and that for some of those traditions the curation of liturgical forms has been close to their polity all along, I hope this book might be useful to others as well. I am thinking in particular of leaders in the Evangelical Lutheran Church in America (our full communion partner), and in the Presbyterian Church (USA) and the United Methodist Church. The ELCA resources are incredibly rich. The Presbyterian *Book of Common Worship*[3] is, in my opinion, one of the very finest of the non-Roman Catholic liturgical resources of the modern period, and the United Methodist Church's book[4] is also a close cousin to ours, as Anglicanism and Methodism themselves are cousins. Even though the use of their authorized resources is not binding on local ecclesial communities in the way that the Episcopal Church's are canonically binding, there are plenty of Presbyterians and Methodists who adopted the principles of the liturgical movement and both the theology and structure of the Eucharist as reflected in the landmark text *Baptism, Eucharist, and Ministry*.[5] This is

---

3. Presbyterian Church USA, *Book of Common Worship* (Louisville: Westminster John Knox Press, 1993 and 2018).

4. Methodist Church, *United Methodist Book of Worship* (Nashville: United Methodist Publishing House, 1992).

5. WCC, Commission on Faith and Order, *Baptism, Eucharist, and Ministry* (Geneva: World Council of Churches, 1982. See also *Baptism, Eucharist, and Ministry, 1982-1990: Report on the Process and Responses* (Geneva: World Council of Churches, 1990).

also the case for other non-Roman churches with polities of local authority that are liturgically literate and have adopted the patterns of Sunday worship represented in the churches with liturgical books. Even leaders in the Roman Catholic Church may find some of the book's provocations cast valuable light on particular practices and ritual structures that characterize their worship life. We are, after all, drawing from the same wells of liturgical renewal to which the Roman Catholic Church has contributed so much. To be sure, for non-Episcopalians to use this book will involve a work of translation, but I hope one that is not terribly difficult. In any case, for non-Episcopalians, Chapters Two, Four, and Five may offer some particular value, though the chapters on best practices comment on Episcopal rites that run parallel to others in our ecumenical family and will, I hope, also be useful.

First then, we turn to an overview of our current moment in the Episcopal Church and how we got here.

1

The Authority of the 1979 Prayer Book and the Currents of Liturgical Change

Long committed to the historic Anglican norm of a single prayer book, the Episcopal Church is now at a liturgical inflection point—one that has a significant impact on liturgical leadership. While committed by canon and by heart to the 1979 *Book of Common Prayer*, the Episcopal Church has for some time been developing supplemental liturgical resources and is encouraging liturgical renewal that includes the possible production of new or revised rites for optional use. Based on recent debates, these revisions and resources may or may not lead to a single new prayer book, at least in the immediate future. Time and testing of the liturgies, and the church's discernment around them, will guide that outcome.

The deliberate revision of our liturgical rites and resources and the range of liturgical options that planners now have calls for particular care on the part of clergy and others responsible for the liturgical life of the Christian assembly, especially on Sunday, "the Lord's Day." Priests in particular, whose Baptismal vocation centers on gathering the liturgical assembly around Book, Font, and Table and leading worship there, find themselves choosing from a sometimes mystifying array of authorized resources to craft the rhythm and content of the assembly's liturgical worship. Certain "givens" remain— for example, the lectionary, though even there some options must be chosen in the season after Pentecost. Priests and others responsible for leadership must *curate* our various liturgical resources like never before, must know how to do so, and, of course, they must *lead well* their congregations and communities in worship. It is my hope that this book will help to clarify the nature of these resources and how to pray well with the prayer book, the new resources, and those still to emerge.

How We Got Here

There was a time—as much a function of romanticism regarding the church's early centuries as of any scholarly rigor—that we imagined a certain unity to the worship across the church that, over time, devolved into a diversity of practices across different regions and cities and (eventually) different churches. That "later" liturgical diversity was often viewed as a kind of loss, a falling away from an early unity of practice. Good historical work, and certainly the historical work of the twentieth century liturgical movement in its unfolding into the twenty first, gradually overturned that romanticism. In fact, we now realize, while there was certainly a sharing of some practices and theologies across the regions into which Christianity spread— perhaps we might think of those as family resemblances—there was a significant degree of diversity in the content of Christian corporate prayer from its very beginning. This appears to us now as unsurprising, sensitive as we are to the fact that all liturgy is contextualized (liturgists often use the term *incultur-ated*), even as it celebrates certain universals of faith and theology. It would make sense, then, that the liturgical practices of a Christian community near Jerusalem, though recognizable to a Christian community in, say, Antioch or Milan, would have its own characteristic features.

In the meantime, while we were learning more about the liturgical unity-in-diversity of the Christian communities of the early centuries, there arose in many other fields and endeavors, including Christian theology, a deepening respect for diversity, for *difference,* not as a falling away from unity, but as a mark of human persons and communities to be cherished and not regretted, and as fundamental to human existence as *unity.* One can detect in late modernity a broad movement in theology toward a recognition that orthodoxy is a frame in which we converse, not the end of the conversation about the faith that we hold. That Jesus Christ, as the very incarnation of God for us, is the one in whom the world is set right, is the central and universal affirmation that makes one Christian and not something else. But the moment one begins to speak about the precise nature of the Incarnation, what it is about the world that needs to be set right, how we are to understand the nature of the remedy God offers in Christ, and so on, we find Christians speaking in many different voices. This is seen to be *good*, and that very diversity is alive in the multiple images and ideas that are rehearsed Sunday by Sunday in liturgy—in fact, our liturgical practice, like Scripture itself, resources the ongoing conversation and testimony that is the living Christian tradition. For a community of four gospels, theological diversity, like liturgical diversity, is taken to be both good and given. How else could it be in a case where language speaks at the limits of its capacity before the Holy One who is at once given to us in a world of language, and beyond all language?

It was in the atmosphere of this broad movement toward a recognition of both *original* diversity in Christian liturgical practice and the *goodness* of liturgical and theological diversity that the 1979 prayer book came into being. The revision of the 1928 prayer book and the path to the 1979 has its own very specific liturgical and theological history. This has been addressed in many other fine books and I will not rehearse the particulars here. But the 1979 book reflects the sense that some diversity in our liturgical-theological resources is an enrichment of Christian life and witness.

Certainly, the 1979 book reflects an ecumenical consensus that we are united around certain structural features of Christian worship that have been with us from the beginning. The Church...

- gathers to hear the Scriptures and pray,
- baptizes both the evangelized and its own youngest members (who will be evangelized in the process of growth and nurturance into their Baptismal identity),
- and celebrates the mystery of our redemption, strengthening us in our Baptismal ministry by the sacraments ...

but it also honors the goodness of a diverse range of liturgical resources in doing so. At this crucial turn, with the 1979 book the Episcopal Church moved from a unity grounded in a single rite—one form for Baptism, one form for Communion, and so forth—to a unity grounded in common ritual structure. While the 1979 prayer book has one rite for Baptism, with some options within it, which it restores to its appropriate place in the public assembly on Sunday, it has a particular variety of forms in other cases. There are two rites for Morning Prayer as well as two rites for the Eucharist with provisions for a more locally planned celebration; and there are many options *within these rites* for certain parts of the service. For some, the most immediate examples of this diversity are in the Holy Eucharist Rite Two which includes several seasonal Acclamations, six different suggestions for the Prayers of the People (and the encouragement to construct these prayers locally), four different Eucharistic Prayers, different forms for Confession and the post-Communion prayer, and so forth. What unites Episcopalians, then, in our Sunday worship, is not the prayer book as *a set of single rites* for Baptism, Eucharist, and so on, but the celebration of the Eucharist *in a common structure* with at least some diversity from one congregation to another.

Among generations prior to the 1979 book, one sometimes heard it said that you could walk into an Episcopal Church anywhere and know that you would encounter the same liturgy as you would be celebrating at home. This was never entirely true. From one parish to the next, there were various choices of hymns and musical settings. The style of ceremonial and vesture and the overall tenor of the service could vary. The liturgy might be Morning Prayer or Holy Communion or both. This does not even touch local inculturated practices or the bearing that differences in the built environment bring to the liturgical celebration. The character of liturgical worship prior to the final authorization of the 1979 book was never *identical* from one Episcopal Church to the next. But in that light, we can see that the 1979 *Book of Common Prayer* actually *embraces* that diversity, *authorizes* it through its forms, and deepens it. At the same time, the 1979 book brings to Episcopal liturgical worship an emerging ecumenical commitment to the Eucharist as the "principal act of Christian worship on the Lord's Day and other major Feasts" (BCP 1979 p. 13), which can be celebrated according to two different rites with a common structure, a variety of options within each rite, and a single Baptismal rite as "full initiation by water and the Holy Spirit.... appropriately administered within the Eucharist as the chief service on a Sunday or other feasts," with a common structure both for the whole rite and for the Eucharistic Prayer, with one exception I will discuss later in the book. Of course, the inclusion of Proper Liturgies for Ash Wednesday through the Great Vigil of Easter is crucial to the theology of Paschal Mystery that characterizes the 1979 prayer book, but I have written on those annual liturgies elsewhere and confine myself here to the Sunday-by-Sunday work of liturgical leadership.[1]

With this understanding of the 1979 prayer book in mind—committed to the centrality of Baptism and Eucharist,

---

1. James Farwell, *This Is the Night: Suffering, Salvation, and the Liturgies of Holy Week* (New York: T&T Clark, 2005); and "Proper Liturgies for Special Days in the 1979 Prayer Book: Considerations in Light of Possible Revision," *Sewanee Theological Review* 61:1 (2017), pp. 193-212. Mitchell's planning guide also remains useful. See Leonel Mitchell, *Lent, Holy Week, Easter, and the Great Fifty Days: A Ceremonial Guide* (Landham: Cowley Publications, 1996).

with a common structure through which diverse forms and their diverse theological images and concepts can be prayed—we acknowledge that curation of liturgical forms is not entirely new. Priests in charge of congregations and lay leaders of worship have been doing the work of curation for some time, but with fewer options for use. What has changed in the current environment is that the *range* of optional resources for use in the standard Eucharistic structure of the Sunday celebration is now *significantly* wider and found not only within the prayer book but also in a number of supplemental resources authorized for use. Add to this the various experimental forms authorized in one way or another by General Convention. The wider this range gets, the more we need to attend carefully to the selection of resources, and the more we need principles for curation. The Episcopal Church is more ethnically, linguistically, and culturally diverse today than it was during the years of the 1928 book, and so such principles will need to take this welcome diversity, too, into account.

The 79th General Convention

The 79th General Convention of the Episcopal Church in 2018 manifests the liturgical inflection point at which we find ourselves. *Its contribution is somewhat ambiguous*, though it becomes a bit more refined and clarified by the recent 80th General Convention. A brief review of the 79th Convention's approach is in order here because it sets the context for the principles and best practices that follow.

Strictly speaking, clergy of the Episcopal Church are obligated to use the prayer book, the other authorized resources of the Episcopal Church (authorized hymnals and musical supplements and texts like, for example, the *Book of Occasional Services* or the volumes of *Enriching our Worship*), and locally developed liturgical resources where the prayer book specifically authorizes such. The polity of the Episcopal Church means that the decision about church-wide liturgical forms is made at its triennial General Convention. In all candor, incremental (and occasionally even profound) liturgical adaptation gets made by clergy even to forms that the prayer book prescribes. Sometimes these adaptations are responsive to the local missional context or culture, sometimes to local pastoral needs, sometimes to the ethnic or racial makeup of a community, sometimes to theological concerns a priest or their community might have about the liturgical forms themselves. Sometimes these changes occur as a groundswell from the assembly itself. Consider how commonly around the Episcopal Church, now, in the opening Acclamation of the Eucharist, "And blessed be his kingdom, now and forever..." is changed to "And blessed be God's kingdom...."[2] This change has emerged as a slow groundswell, motivated by sensitivity to unnecessary gender bias in language referring to God, and it is widespread probably because it is largely unobjectionable, losing nothing of the meaning of the original form while gaining the gender neutrality. (Other proposed changes to liturgical language are far more contested.)

In the best case, liturgical practices that do not follow

---

2. The expansive language rendering of Rite II authorized by General Convention in 2018 codifies this common change as follows: "...and blessed be God's reign...." More will follow on the expansive language Rite II in Chapter 3.

the prayer book and are not authorized by the church should be implemented by clergy only after long prayer and deeply informed, conscientious reflection on our liturgical and sacramental theology, a compelling argument for why the authorized form should not be followed, and permission from the bishop. (There is some difference of opinion on the extent of the change that our Constitution and Canons or prayer book rubrics authorize a bishop to make, but someone else can write that book!) In the regrettable worst case, changes are made by clergy on a whim, a personal preference, or a response to a fad, or are driven by the personality of the presider rather than sound liturgical reasoning.

Beyond these particular cases of adaptation that may go beyond what is authorized by the prayer book, changes to authorized forms naturally tend to increase as time passes after the authorization of a new prayer book, and so does the sense that the prayer book needs revision. Going into the 79th General Convention, there was much debate across the church about whether it is time for prayer book revision. Some members of the church argued that we are ready for revision; others argued that we had only begun to live deeply into the Baptismal emphasis of the 1979 book and need more time for formation into that theology. Some worried that the church would be consumed by prayer book revision when it should be focusing on evangelization and revitalization. (I might say, with regret, that some making that argument fail to see the intrinsic connections between the welcome of the newcomer and the centrality of liturgical practice to the formation of the community into which the newcomer is welcomed.)

The 79th General Convention, faced with a resolution to begin the process of revision, produced in the end a compromise approach. The final text of the resolution, GC 2018-A068, is worth some close attention in light of this book's purpose.

Resolution 2018 – A068

Resolved, That the 79th General Convention, pursuant to Article X of the Constitution, authorize the ongoing work of liturgical and Prayer Book revision for the future of God's mission through the Episcopal branch of the Jesus movement. And, that it do so upon the core theological work of loving, liberating, life-giving reconciliation and creation care; and be it further

Resolved, That our methodology be one of a dynamic process for discerning common worship, engaging all the baptized, while practicing accountability to The Episcopal Church; and be it further

Resolved, That the 79th General Convention create a Task Force on Liturgical and Prayer Book Revision (TFLPBR), the membership of which will be jointly appointed by the Presiding Bishop and the President of the House of Deputies, and will report to the appropriate legislative committee(s) of the 80th General Convention, ensuring that diverse voices of our church are active participants in this liturgical revision by constituting a group with leaders who represent the expertise, gender, age, theology, regional, and ethnic diversity of the church, to include, 10 laity, 10 priests or deacons, and 10 Bishops; and be it further

Resolved, That this Convention memorialize the 1979 Book of Common Prayer as a Prayer Book of the church preserving the psalter, liturgies, The Lambeth Quadrilateral, Historic Documents, and Trinitarian Formularies ensuring its continued use; and be it further

Resolved, That this church continue to engage the deep Baptismal and Eucharistic theology and practice of the 1979 Prayer Book; and be it further

Resolved, That bishops engage worshiping communities in experimentation and the creation of alternative texts to offer to the wider church, and that each diocese be urged to create a liturgical commission to collect, reflect, teach and share these resources with the TFLPBR; and be it further

Resolved, That the TFLPBR in consultation with the Standing Commission on Structure, Governance, Constitution and Canons is directed to propose to the 80th General Convention revisions to the Constitution and Canons to enable The Episcopal Church to be adaptive in its engagement of future generations of Episcopalians, multiplying, connecting, and disseminating new liturgies for mission, attending to Prayer Book revision in other provinces of the Anglican Communion; and be it further

Resolved, That liturgical and Prayer Book revision will continue in faithful adherence to the historic rites of the Church Universal as they have been received and interpreted within the Anglican tradition of 1979 Book of Common Prayer, mindful of our existing ecumenical commitments, while also providing space for, encouraging the submission of, and facilitating the perfection of rites that will arise from the continual movement of the Holy Spirit among us and growing insights of our Church; and be it further

Resolved, That such revision utilize the riches of Holy Scripture and our Church's liturgical, cultural, racial, generational, linguistic, gender, physical ability, class and ethnic diversity in order to share common worship; and be it further

Resolved, That our liturgical revision utilize inclusive and expansive language and imagery for humanity and divinity; and be it further

Resolved, That our liturgical revision shall incorporate and express understanding, appreciation, and care of God's creation; and be it further

Resolved, That our liturgical revision take into consideration the use of emerging technologies which provide access to a broad range of liturgical resources; and be it further

Resolved, That the SCLM create a professional dynamic equivalence translation of the Book of Common Prayer 1979 and the Enriching Our Worship Series in Spanish, French, and Haitian Creole; and that the SCLM diversify the publication formats of new resources, liturgies and rites to include online publishing; and be it further

Resolved, That this church ensure that, at each step of the revision process, all materials be professionally translated into English, Spanish, French, and Haitian Creole, following the principles of dynamic equivalence and that no new rites or liturgical resources be approved by this church until such translations are secured....

Clauses 1 and 2 frame prayer book revision as an "ongoing work," and rightfully links liturgical renewal to mission—as

I noted above, *liturgy and mission are not two separate items on a list of things that the church does but are instead integrally related.* Gathering for worship is both the effect of God's mission in the world and formation for our deepening participation in it. This is quite consistent with the core theology of the 1979 prayer book, that of "Paschal Mystery," the participation of the church in Christ through the ongoing work of the Spirit who speaks through the Word and sanctifies both the people who gather and the meal that they eat together. The first clause also makes reference to Article X of our Constitution, to which an amendment to "authorize for use throughout this church, as provided by Canon, alternative and additional liturgies to supplement those provided in the Book of Common Prayer" is making its way through legislation.[3] This creates a constitutional legitimacy to supplemental liturgies which do not fall in the category of trial rites (which become part of the "next" prayer book). The second clause is, in my view, likely a response to an unsupportable claim that is parroted in some circles today: that the 1979 prayer book was the work of liturgical scholars and dropped unannounced on the heads of those in the pews. In fact, the 1979 book emerged from a church wide process of praying with trial rites. (To be sure, in some places, church leaders did not do the work of educating or using the trial rites, so that when the 1979 book was approved, the impression was that it had been a production of scholars without consultation. However, in plenty of dioceses there was a process of catechesis around an exploration of the new

---

3. See clause c of resolution A063 in the journal of the 2018 General Convention, and A059 in the summary of actions of the 2022 General Convention.

rites, and a careful process of feedback on their use, so it was clear that the "new" book was the work of the whole church.) The second stanza is nevertheless a welcome reminder that liturgical revisions can only be tested by being prayed, and it is the whole church that should be involved in the praying and perhaps even some drafting, while liturgical scholars also bring to bear their expertise within the process.

Clause 3 of resolution A068 establishes an interim body whose purpose is not entirely clear from the clause itself. The task force is to be diverse, and balanced across various categories, but whether they are to gather and assess liturgical experiments already underway, develop principles, or actually develop proposals or rites is not specified. However, clause 6 sharpens the task by placing the responsibility for the gathering and/or development of new rites in the hands of the dioceses, guided by their bishops, so it would seem that the primary task of the interim body appointed in clause 3 is to gather those resources and, with some assessment of them, to report back their findings to the 80th General Convention. How exactly the dioceses are to do this work appears left to bishops to determine. But the appointment of the task force does it make it quite clear that some liturgical revision is now underway, and more lies ahead of us.

At the same time, the very next clause (4) "memorializes" the 1979 prayer book as "a Prayer Book of the church." "Memorialization" is an ambiguous concept and often derives its meaning from the context in which it is offered. It is imprecise here and has caused no small amount of comment around the church. With the use of the phrase "a" rather than "the" prayer book, it seems to denote only that the 1979 book continues to be authorized for use but expresses nothing regarding its normativity, which is left to other constitutional commitments. This does insure that the 1979 book is not simply cast aside. When this clause is set together with clauses 5 and 8, the effect of the total resolution is a bit less ambiguous: the Episcopal Church commits itself to continue in the theology and ecclesiology of the 1979 book (that the church participates in the very mystery of Christ through Baptism, nourished by sacred bread and wine, to grow ever more deeply into Christ's own body, sharing in his priesthood as witnesses to Christ in the world). Reading these stanzas together, it is clear that the 1979 book remains *theologically* normative, and it suggests that other liturgical resources are likely, though not required, to function supplementally to the full collection of rites in the 1979 book, similar to the way in which the resources of the first volume of the *Enriching Our Worship* series has been designed and utilized.

Resolution A068 is illuminating in one other way: it gathers into the one resolution the most prominent concerns for revision that have been driving liturgical proposals in recent years. Those concerns include lifting up the diversity of the church (clause 9), developing more expansive language for both God and humanity (clause 10), and fostering the stewardship of creation (clause 11). A commitment to dynamic translations, better than we have produced in the past, is a significant support to the realization of the diversity noted in clause 9. New materials to be curated by liturgical leaders going forward will reflect one or more of these concerns, and curators might best do their choosing among options with these concerns in mind. Care will need to be taken in determining their usage in ways that extend the theology of the 1979 book while remaining rooted within it.[4]

80th General Convention

In July 2022 (delayed one year by the SARS-CoV2 pandemic), General Convention moved along the shift set by 2018-A068, in 2022-A057, directing the Standing Commission on Liturgy and Music (SCLM) to "continue the work of liturgical and Prayer Book revision," using *Principles to Guide the Development of Liturgical Texts* articulated by the SCLM in their report to the Convention.[5] The third stanza was crucial to understanding the process:

> *Resolved,* That bishops continue to engage worshiping communities in experimentation and the creation of alternative texts to offer to the wider church, and diocesan liturgical commissions collect and share these resources with the SCLM, and that the SCLM review these resources and materials submitted… for consideration in the process of liturgical and Prayer Book revision.

This keeps the bishops at the hinge point between the development of local texts and rites and their communication

---

4. There are a range of responses to 2018-A068 by scholars of the Anglican Consortium of the North American Academy of Liturgy in a collection edited by Stephanie Budwey, Kevin Moroney, Sylvia Sweeney, and Samuel Torvend entitled *In Spirit and in Truth: A New Vision of Episcopal Worship* (New York: Church Publishing, 2020).

5. This can be found in the General Convention Blue Book 2021 under the SCLM's report. https://www.generalconvention.org/bluebook2021

with the SCLM, appropriately so, though it must be said that it remains unclear how this would unfold in every diocese, or whether all bishops place a priority on this work, so there is some risk of unevenness in liturgical growth across the church. The SCLM is further charged in this resolution to review the materials that were cultivated in the last triennium by the task force that was created by 2018-A068. A resolution was also passed (2022-A058) to make of episcopalcommonprayer. org, a website created as a place for the task force to lodge its work, the "official liturgical website of the Episcopal Church." This follows the practice by others, including our communion partner the ELCA, of placing liturgical resources online. It will be important for curators to make regular use of that website, although the website itself, as it stands in this moment in time, will need some attention in order to make clear what is authorized and what is there simply to inspire and provoke.

The SCLM is also to make a comprehensive review of all our current liturgical resources with an eye to "colonialist, racist and white supremacist, imperialistic and nationalistic language and content" and to do so by convening persons of color and a variety of ethnicities to develop proposals for any amendments that are necessary (2022-A126). Other resolutions, in the sum total of their effect, make the rites of the prayer book completely interchangeable, such that Rite I in contemporary language becomes a trial rite and (2022-D061) and that all elements of our liturgical materials are interchangeable in this regard. Along with an expansive language version of Rite II authorized for trial use at the 79th Convention and an expansive language version of Rite II Prayer C (2022-A015), found in Appendices B and C, and the direction to make dynamic equivalent translations of all these materials, the resources we have become as elastic as we have ever known.

There were many other resolutions passed at both Conventions regarding liturgy. Some are quite important and widely applicable to the church's liturgical life, many more are appropriate to particular communities, places, and times. I do not linger over them in this book, not because they are insignificant but because my scope here is the Sunday-by-Sunday liturgical life of the church. These other resolutions and resources would require a whole book in themselves.

Interim Conclusions for the Planner and Presider

I offer three interim conclusions about where we now stand in the journey of liturgical revision and renewal. First, the curator and planner of liturgy in today's Episcopal Church will want to make decisions with a high premium on the expression of the church's diversity, on language that makes space for all people in worship, and on our awareness of our place in creation. These are chief among the concerns of the Episcopal Church in this day when racism, ethnic bias, and violence against our neighbors is on the rise, when the full inclusion of all genders is still unfinished business in the church and in the world, and when the natural world of which we are members is in mortal peril. Authentic liturgy will reflect these features of our concrete reality in which our people worship.

At the same time, we will need to remember that liturgy is not a tool for policymaking or forwarding any particular agenda; it is, in fact, not a tool but an end in itself, since in liturgy we enact and enjoy though our praise and prayer the very reconciliation with God that we preach and seek for all people. I will say a bit more in the next chapter about the nature of liturgy as an end in itself.

Second, the curator and planner of liturgy today will need to be especially clear in communication with the bishop to whom they are responsible. That means understanding the bishop's authorizations regarding liturgical uses. There are many new resources now authorized but these do not sidestep the bishop's authority (and responsibility!) for liturgical practice, the vitality of the diocese, and its unity with the wider church. It is the bishop who has a view to the whole diocese and to its liturgical practices. It also means communicating well to the bishop through whatever means they appoint about what liturgical practices occur in one's own context. The developments at General Convention that we reviewed above make it important for the bishop to know what experimentation is happening in the local context, especially with trial rites and supplemental resources, and how they are being received and being prayed. This is a delicate moment we are in: it could produce a flowering of liturgical practice befitting the beautiful diversity of God's world—a unity in diversity. It could also lead to such a dizzying array of different practices that our liturgies cease to be common prayer and our liturgical theology loses its center of gravity in the Pasch.

Thirdly, there is a great danger in the move away from a single book, and that danger is clericalism. Clergy are, rightfully and deliberately, informed by their studies of the history, theology, and performance of liturgy, and much weight now lies upon them to make decisions among a wide range of possible resources. The average, even well-educated layperson will not keep up with all these forms, nor would the time given to their own Baptismal ministries in the world allow for this. Combined with the fact that many of our resources are now lodged in various booklets and on websites, it is going to be the case, more and more, that worship is done with full-text bulletins in which the parts of the liturgy come from several different sources. In a church eager to participate in this liturgical renewal, a single service could commonly come from the prayer book, a volume of *Enriching Our Worship*, the *Book of Occasional Services*, a trial rite authorized by General Convention, and some local construction. The risk, here, is that no one except the priest knows where the liturgy comes from, and the laity become passive in their reception of these forms. This must be prevented. The only way to do so is through the effective use of worship committees, public communication by the priest, education, and regular corporate reflection on worship. Little trumps the importance of ongoing liturgical education for the whole congregation's sense of the ownership of liturgical practice and their sense of belonging in a church reflecting actively on its practices.

I will offer some additional thoughts about what guides the curators and planners of liturgy in the Episcopal Church in Chapter Four. Let us turn now to the features of ritualization that we do well to remember in our liturgical curation and leadership.

2

Ritual and Liturgy

I n a context where presiders can avail ourselves of a number of liturgical resources and must make choices—even if using only the 1979 prayer book!—it is incumbent on us to remember what rituals are and how they work. We flourish in the world when, among other things, we learn to attend to what things are and accommodate ourselves to their natures. A Hamanishi print is a beautiful thing, but if you try to use it to cut a cake, you will not have much success. Ritual, it turns out, is much closer to the Hamanishi than to the cake knife—an end in itself and a work of art. As I said above, we will want to make ritual decisions that go with and not against the grain of rituality.

Ritual literacy is under pressure these days from a number of directions. One is demographic decline. In response, liturgical planners often find themselves tempted to imagine that the primary function of the Sunday assembly is to attract newcomers, to hold the attention of those who are there, to do certain things with ritual—to inspire, excite, attract, and the like—to compensate for, reverse, or fight back against that decline.

This pressure comes to bear in a late modern culture in which instrumentalism and consumerism absorb everything—religion included—into a world of commodities, preferences, a culture in which there is no end that is an end in itself. Everything must be *for* something else, obtain something, satisfy something, achieve something, excite something— preferably, wherever possible, measurable in a quantitative sense, and monetized. In a consumer culture also keyed to spectacle, everything is a product, and must be of sufficient dazzle to sell.

Certainly, we want our liturgical worship to be as winsome as it can be, and liturgy done well has always had the capacity, while being what it is intended to be, to be evangelical in an "attractional" sense as well. The opposite is also true. Doing liturgy in which the readers read the Scripture with a yawn, intercessions sound like lines from a phone book, and the presider seems to be encountering the liturgy as if he or she has never done it before, or reads the prayers out of the book rather than *praying the prayers* that the book provides, can drive away the most well-formed Christian to prefer whatever they might have done at home to a public gathering with no sense of excellence in the doing. However, when we begin to imagine that if we can just do a certain kind of ritual, or the presider can be just compelling enough, or the old service can be retired for something that is always new and dazzling, it will somehow signal our authenticity and attractiveness, we are on the wrong track. Too many celebrity church leaders these days pride themselves on dismissing this or that aspect of the prayer book—or the prayer book itself!—or our other authorized rites as if by their own improvisational worship and sheer charisma they will bring about the reversal of demographic trends.

Here is the rub: ritual is not a commodity; done well, at

times it may indeed please, excite, or fulfill (and may also challenge and convict), but it is not *for* these things. It is not for a payoff, fulfillment or inspiration. It is not designed to produce an experience though we will have some experience of it. Ritual is not an *instrument*; done well, it will form and educate and shape my imagination, but it is not *for* those things. Aim to make ritual a pedagogical or entertainment or inspirational exercise and you will no longer be doing ritual, nor will ritual substitute for the various forms unique to those other activities.

What *is* ritual then? Let me offer some general observations about the nature of ritual and ritualization so that we might practice it well, first distinguishing it from some other related terms. I will then try and draw together what these features of ritual mean for the good curator and presider of Christian liturgy. A reminder: if you would like a more technical and academic grounding for the following observations, you will find some satisfaction in the books recommended in Appendix A.

Worship, Liturgy, Ritual

Ritual needs to be distinguished from other terms to which it is related. The first is "worship." "Worship" by itself is a term with wide application. Among its uses, "worship" can refer broadly to an action or it can refer to an experience—either an experience of an action or a sense that one has of a moment, or takes away from a moment. One can worship through the structured activity of ritual, and one can worship without any particular structure. There are many ways that an individual or a community can worship, and a broad account of worship is not what I am up to here.

"Liturgy" too is distinguished from "ritual," though in a bit different way than "worship" is distinguished from ritual. "Liturgy" is a term we use *for* our rituals. This *interprets* the rituals in a particular way. The term is borrowed by Christians from Hellenistic Roman usage, as the Greek speaking Jews in Roman territories did as well. A liturgy was a public work, a service to the public, to its good or its functioning or its flourishing. The Greek-speaking Jews applied the term to the high priest in his capacity to perform ritual atonement for the people, and Christian Scripture applies the term to service (in the New Testament letters) and to Jesus himself (in Hebrews), in his saving work for the people. "Liturgy," then, is an irreducibly *theological* term. It refers to the "public work" that God has done for the world through Christ, and to apply the term to our rituals of worship is to suggest that through our worship we enter into both the gift and the call of God in Christ. The terms "liturgy" and "Paschal Mystery" are thus congruent with each other: each refers to a participation in Christ, a communion with God entered into through the Spirit's power that extends the reconciliation of God and the world through Christ.

An End in Itself

Ritual, by which I mean the activity of ritualization, is not a specifically Christian activity. Ritual is fundamental to human existence, from as far back in time of which we have record and across all cultures of which we are aware. It is as fundamental to being human as is *play*. In fact, this parallel is quite instructive, because ritual is very much like structured play, and like play, it is not *for* something other than itself. It is an end in itself. We know that play, in the process of its doing, accomplishes many things too: social bonding and training in sociality and cooperation, practice in contestation, the development of spatial and motor skills, and many more. Play accomplishes these things, but it is not *for* these things. From the standpoint of the one playing, the play is the *end in itself*. Even playing at games that involve winning and losing are about more than the winning and losing; they are about the play.

The first feature of ritual we want to note is that, like play, *it is an end in itself*. Like play, there are also other things that happen when we ritualize. We expand our imagination, we are formed and shaped toward particular virtues, particular ways of being in the world and away from other ways of being. Our sense of social cohesion is deepened. We learn. But the ritual is not *for* any of those things. It is its own end. It does all those things by our simply giving ourselves over to it—its extraordinary range of imagery, its rhythm, its content.

This structural characteristic of ritual as an end in itself is in fundamental congruence with the Christian theological account of our rituals as *liturgy*.[1] At the heart of the Christian gospel is the reconciliation of God, humanity, and world. In liturgy, through the modes of praise and prayer, thanksgiving,

---

1. Other religions have their own ways of thinking about the relationship between ritual and religious content, and about ritual as an enacting end in itself. See, e.g., Taigen Dan Leighton, "Zazen as Enactment Ritual," in *Zen Ritual: Studies of Zen Buddhist Theory in Practice*, ed. by Steven Heine (Oxford: Oxford University Press, 2008), pp. 167-184.

intercession, and confession, we stand reconciled in that very act. In communion, in communication, in openness to the divine presence we enact in liturgy the very participation in God that is the proper end of humanity: reconciled, and such reconciliation an end in itself. To be reconciled to God has many effects and many demands. Through our rituals, we are entering into the mission of God in the world. It is a participation in the One whom we worship, an entering into the mystery of God's self-givenness for the world's redemption. The liturgy enacts our *consent* to be caught up in the mission of God in the world, centered on the redemptive power of the death and resurrection of Christ. But all of these things that liturgy does, it does when we enter the liturgy as the telos of human existence: in this life, seeing through a glass darkly, enacting communion with God. This is what is behind the well-known line from Roman Catholic documents in the Second Vatican Council: the liturgy, an end in itself, is both "source and summit" of our Christian life.[2]

Bodily Action

The second characteristic of ritual is its bodily nature. Ritual is full-body action, using all the senses. As human beings who are material and finite in our very identity, ritual will always involve the whole body in its work. There are acts of cognition that occur as part of ritual action, and there are words said and heard, but these too are in fact bodily actions. Ritual takes seriously that human beings know with the whole body, and not just with the mind—something the modern period

---

2. *The Catechism of the Catholic Church*, sect. 1324.

has tended to forget, though many disciplines are now revisiting the significant connections between body and mind. In connection with this embodied cognition, the *space* in which the assembly stands and kneels, walks and bows, is of high importance in ritual. In fact, the built environment in which ritual occurs contributes significant force to the action.

It bears lingering on this point about material space just a little. It is true that the church is the people of God, not the building in which the church gathers for its liturgy. It never takes long in a conversation on liturgical space for someone to say, "Well, why all this concern with space? The church can worship anywhere!" Someone is sure to bring up the fact in such a moment that the early church did its liturgy in houses. This is an indisputable fact. What is equally an indisputable fact is that, from the beginning of human history, human beings engaged in ritual action have either modified space or built space dedicated to ritual action. Engaging in common space for sacred activity is generally a short-lived affair, until dedicated space can be built or made. Christians were no exception. Architectural evidence suggests that the houses used for Christian gatherings were also early on *modified* for that purpose. In the case of Christian ritual, what rises to prominence from this early trajectory of space usage was a place for the Scriptures to be read, neophytes to be baptized, and sufficient space for the meal to be held. The three spaces that James White called "liturgical centers" today—Ambo, Font, and Altar/Table—are the anchor points of the assembly's meeting. At the Font, we join Christ's Body, the Church, in its new life in Christ; at the Ambo, we are addressed and called by the presence of Christ through the Word; and at the Altar, we are sustained by the presence of Christ in the Sacrament and strengthened for Baptismal service in his name.

It is, finally, important that the rituals that concern us are *corporate* bodily action. It makes a difference that we hear *together* from the same holy book, eat *together* from the same holy Table. The very nature of the reconciliation that ritual enacts is a reconciliation with God and therefore... and thereby ... with one another. One of the two oldest theologies of the Eucharist in the Christian tradition is that through and by the eating together we are made one. Corporate ritual action puts flesh on the bones of that theology.

Repetition

The actions undertaken in and through bodies in our rituals are repetitive. Repetition is of course a familiar part of our lives, and not all repetition constitutes a ritual. Our days are marked by many repetitive actions and those with a taste for fine-tuned anthropology can spend a fair amount of time looking for the line where routine crosses over into ritual. Occasionally we even use the words interchangeably—one might have said, at some point, "I have completed my morning ritual." Where repetition is routine and where it is ritual is something we can leave the ritual anthropologists to argue out; for our purposes, we can say this at least: repetition is an essential part of how we keep our days, even who we are. Repetition may be pointless in some cases, but in many other cases, repetition is significant: it marks our vocations, it maintains activity essential to our health, and it often reveals what is most important to us. While novelty also has its value and other purposes, in repetition we return again and again to something that becomes important, rightly or wrongly, *by the returning.* Its importance in ritual may be seen by connecting it to two other features of ritual: structure and orientation.

Structure and Orientation

Ritual might be described as structured repetition oriented to high value. For a religious tradition, the orientation is to *transcendent* value. Religions differ, of course, on what is considered transcendent, and how the transcendent is related to the ordinary. Even within one tradition, including our own, the transcendent (God) in relationship to the ordinary might be accounted for in a number of different ways, which are funded by the diverse content of our faith that appears in our liturgies. The content of ritual action—what we say, sing, and pray—is of great importance and in due course I will turn to that too. But we do not want to overlook the significance of structure and its repetition.

Augustine once defined a sacrament as sign set next to word.[3] Gordon Lathrop, the contemporary Lutheran scholar of liturgy, has noted that liturgy as a whole arises from the setting of one thing next to another in complex ways. At the level of the most fundamental elements of liturgy, Lathrop argues, it is the setting next to one another of Word, Bath, Table, and Prayer.[4] It is also true that the order of the entire service, what comes first and what comes next, the order in

---

3. Augustine, *Tractates on the Gospel of John*, tractate 80, sec. 3.
4. Gordon W. Lathrop, *Holy Ground: A Liturgical Cosmology* (Minneapolis: Fortress Press, 1999), p. 224.

which things are set next to one another, is also significant to what is being enacted there as we orient ourselves to the transcendent Holy One. We will see, in the practices below, that it is immensely important for the presider to know *in their bones* the structure-in-motion of the liturgy. That we gather, then hear the Word, then go to the Table, then move into the World... that in gathering we begin with acknowledgement of God and sing, and only then pray; that in hearing the Word, we both listen and respond; that at the Table we give thanks through remembrance before we invoke the Spirit and receive; that in going, we go quickly... There are several overlapping rhythms here, which I will designate with Alexander Schmemann's term *ordo*,[5] and all these rhythms are in motion in the *structure* of the rite and have everything to do with what the ritual action means, because what the ritual *means* is what it *does*.

I linger here over ritual as repetitive structure because this is a tough one, it seems, for us moderns. Modernity places very high value on the new, the fresh, the latest update, the next advancement. We planners and presiders can slip into the assumption that liturgy too must be different each time we gather, and in so doing, work against the fact that ritual works in large part through its structural repetition.

This repetition is closely related to familiarity. Not every element of a ritual is or must be familiar, but a notable portion of the ritual will be. Here, not only structure but content is implicated. While in Christian ritual there is content that

---

5. Alexander Schmemann, *Introduction to Liturgical Theology* (Crestwood, NY: Saint Vladimir's Seminary Press, 1996), pp. 33ff.

changes from week to week, there are set pieces that occur not only at the same time but in the same words and actions. Getting the relationship between change and familiar repetition just right is partly received from the tradition, but also the outcome of the planner's art.

Reception

Speaking of what is received from the tradition: in an important way, tradition *is* reception. We receive the tradition by setting it into motion through our liturgical action. But the sense that we are receiving something that we did not simply create out of whole cloth is an important dimension of ritual action. We do know that our rituals did not drop from the sky. Nor are they phenomena occurring in nature. Our ancestors have been worshiping with similar forms, and the generations before us revised and formalized the rituals we use, drawing in turn from those that went before them. So we are part of a community that created these rituals, yet this sense that these rituals are received from those who have gone before is part of their authority for us, and that authority in turn gives them power. In important ways we *consent* to the rituals we enact, and that consent lives in and as the authorized ritual's performance. This is an important part of the power of ritual for us—that we receive these forms, even as we contribute to their doing.

Performance

Rituals are scripted activity, but the ritual is not the script. It is a performance. Its meaning is in the doing. The structure and content of the ritual is performed, typically in a space (whether natural or built) dedicated to it, usually on a calendar of performance that shapes the content. But the ritual's power is in the doing, over time, in the space. As I will note below, this is why the art of ritual leadership is so crucial. While ritual accomplished without energy can still accomplish its meaning, and while ritual led in an overly affected manner may interfere but not entirely nullify the experience of the ritual, artful leadership of ritual is done in such a way that the script of the ritual is brought alive as ritual performance, neither led like one is reading a phone book, nor dramatized as if it will only be effective if the leader is dramatic.

Ordinary...and Not

While rituals may use certain specialized objects, the most fundamental objects in ritual are on a continuum with naturally occurring objects and activities in ordinary life. The Baptismal Font is like a bath, and Baptism a bathing; the Altar is like a table, and Communion, though not only or primarily a meal, is a meal. Ritual thus performs what is holy and sacred, enacts human destiny in communion with God not in a separate realm from the ordinary, but in and among the ordinary. This is true of most all religious ritual across cultures, but it is particularly appropriate to an Incarnational faith that celebrates God's redemption of the world by God's entering into it.

Multivalence

My last observation about ritual is about its content. In the observations above I have for the most part focused on what is stable, repetitive, and familiar about ritual. Much of that has to do with structure, though the structure is always composed of something. Here, a note on that *something*.

The content of ritual falls in two general classes. One can be thought of as content that is invariable. For example, in the Episcopal Eucharistic rite there is an element of the rite we can describe as "response to the Word proclaimed." One of those is the Nicene Creed. (The other two are intercessory prayer and, most times of the year, a Confession and absolution and the sharing of the Peace with one another.) Our rubrics specify that the Nicene Creed is always said as an assembly as a response to the Word on Sundays and Major Feasts. This is an example of a fixed element in the rite that provides content—very specifically, the voicing of an ancient creedal formulation about the relationship between Jesus Christ, the Holy Spirit, and the creator God. Immediately following that Creed, however, are intercessions. There will always *be* intercessions (the "Prayers of the People"), and they will always touch on specified concerns (the nation and its leaders, the sick, etc.), but the content of those intercessions can—and one might say, should—vary from week to week. The content of the rite that changes, or most commonly changes, weekly are the Collect of the Day, the lections appointed for the day, the Sermon, the Prayers of the People, the preface of the Great Thanksgiving (if the Eucharistic Prayer is one that uses a "variable" preface), and the music used, which plays a role both by the lyrics of the hymns, but also what we might call the "mood," a function of melody, key, tempo, and the like.

All these variable elements of a ritual occur at specified places in the ritual script. Thus, they are both fixed in the sense that they do certain "works" in the sequence, but they also bring a variety of ideas and images into the action. This multivalence both funds and expresses the Christian imagination of the kingdom of God—that is, of the destiny of the human person in reconciled relation to creator and creation. In all this, its structure and sequence, its variability and multivalence, its rhythm and performance, we enact in ritual a way of being before God: in awe before the holy, grateful for gifts of God including life itself and grace, open to God's speech and silence, attentive to suffering and need, prepared to make peace with one another, receiving sustenance from God's hand, oriented toward the world in grateful witness.

Implications for the Curator, Planner, Presider

More can be said of ritual and its key features (and has been!) but those I have touched on are some of the most important to bear in mind. To summarize, there is ritual's structure and sequence, its content both fixed and variable, its familiarity and repetition over time and in space as a corporate action whose meaning is in its doing, an end in itself as it enacts in ritual form the reconciled relationship of God and all creation. What does all this mean for the curator of forms, the planner of liturgies, the presider over the assembly's liturgical worship?

The wise curator of liturgical forms does not move too rapidly through their use. Ritual *structure* does not change, or changes little,[6] but when it comes to planning the variable content of the rites, the *pieces* of the structure if you will, the default orientation should be for *stability* and evolution that is slow and steady. The lections will change week to week according to their own cycle; the Intercessions should change, if not weekly, at least fairly often. (More on that below.) But the power of ritual, and its capacity to model in our performance of it a particular way of being before God—reconciled, in communion, transformed or at least being transformed—is a function of the stability, recognizability, repetition of ritual practice. So too is the *authority* of liturgy, its power to work on us over time, a function of its repetition. Eventually, if many things change from week to week, the ritual ceases to be ritual and becomes the product of the planner's creativity. In the attention economy in which we live, the ritual will now be subject to the question of how appealing, how interesting, how different it is from one gathering to the next. Once this door is opened, ritual is lost, and the work of liturgy quickly becomes a high-minded form of entertainment.

For the liturgical planner, there is the need to choose the variable forms and music as appropriate to the context and in a way that the rite moves in accordance with its own structure. For example: processional music should serve the movement of the leaders into the space, of a character that suits the note of the entrance rite within its season, and neither so short as to fail to prime the assembly for prayer nor so long that is gives

---

6. E.g., the common practice of using the Penitential Rite for the Eucharist during Lent (BCP 351) changes the elements *within* the entrance rite but does not eliminate the entrance rite of the liturgy *per se*, or change the general structure that it follows.

more weight to the entrance rite than is its purpose: to get the assembly into place for the proclamation of the Word, which along with the Sacrament is the center of gravity of the event. Eucharistic Prayers should be selected with the calendar of the church and the context of the assembly in mind. Even there, too much speed in cycling through options will limit the power of a particular prayer to fund, form, and express the horizon of the assembly's life.

For the presider, it is crucial to know the structure and rhythm in liturgy in their bones and move the assembly along with it, as it is in the assembly's performance that the rite comes to life. A presider must move not too fast and not so slow; too fast makes the performance a matter of rote business; too slow and the sequence ceases to move, the assembly cannot feel its meaning-in-motion. Presiders must also beware perhaps the most common error in liturgical churches: instead of praying the script, they read it. A presider standing at the Altar is not *reading* a prayer any more than in preaching they are *reading* a Sermon or in the assembly's singing they are analyzing a musical score. Unfortunately we have all seen this happen. The presider as a member of the assembly is to *pray* and to *preach*, not simply read. This embodies an invitation to the assembly that they too, will not simply read their parts, but pray. The Presider must also attend to the various forms of speech in a ritual script: there is exhortation, bidding, proclamation, prayer, invocation, and so on, and each of these is led or voiced in a way particular to the nature of the form. For the ritual to be fully authentic and fully powerful as *worship*, it is to be performed, and performed as an end in itself. Such sincerity and care is a gift of grace, such intentionality only possible in humility. For these qualities we presiders pray both in and beyond the liturgy. By this we may praise well and give thanks with a gravity befitting the truth we celebrate. The rest of ritual's functions, secondary and ancillary to this primary work—to educate, to inspire, to convict—will take care of themselves.

3

Curating Resources in the Episcopal Church

W hen we consider the resources that we curate as liturgical planners, we begin, of course, with the 1979 *Book of Common Prayer*. As noted in Chapter One, the 1979 book already represents a resource that requires a *curation* of its forms—a departure in large part from previous books. There is a single rite for Baptism, but with some options around the order of handlaying and Chrismation, the post-Baptismal prayer, and the Prayers of the People. When it comes to the "mainframe" of the Sunday liturgy, we have before us seasonal options for the Acclamation and choices to make for music during the times when a Song of Praise can replace the Gloria; four options for Eucharistic Prayers, with some choice for variable Prefaces during certain seasons for those Eucharistic Prayers that allow for them; alternatives for the post-Communion prayer; and more. Of course, there is the choice between a rite in an updated Tudor idiom and a rite in the formal vernacular—Rite I and Rite II. Any of the modern language prayers may be used in Rite I as well, changed to the Tudor idiom. (Although the exercise of that option has been relatively rare in the Episcopal Church, I will discuss below what commends that option for those communities who continue, whatever their reasons, to use Rite I; and I will discuss what General Convention just resolved in this regard as well.) There is also in the 1979 prayer book some material that is commonly, though quite erroneously, known as "Rite Three." This is the material on page 400ff. of the prayer book, which presents the necessary order in which a community might plan and offer Eucharist not using either of the two rites available. What it shows is the structure of the Eucharist that lives within Rite I and II, and this structure is normative.

A number of resources have been authorized since 1979 to supplement the authorized book. These include the *Book of Occasional Services* (hereafter BOS), *Lesser Feasts and Fasts* (hereafter LFF) and the *Enriching Our Worship* series (hereafter EOW)—five volumes of "expansive language" material that augment the options for many (though not all) of the elements of the prayer book rites as well as providing some new materials. EOW volume 1 contains an updated Great Litany, a number of new Canticles for Morning Prayer (which also supplement the resources for the Song of Praise in the entrance rite), and new resources for several elements of the prayer book's Eucharistic liturgy. Of the latter, among the most significant in my view are additional Acclamations and options for opening Collects, an additional way of introducing and concluding the reading of Scripture, a modified Nicene Creed, another form for Confession, three new Eucharistic Prayers, and two more post-Communion prayers.[1]

---

1. EOW has a companion volume with new musical settings for the Canticles. See *Enriching Our Music* (New York: Church Publishing, 2003).

In addition to authorizing EOW, General Convention has now given us an expansive language form of the entire Rite II liturgy, excluding Eucharistic Prayer C, and then, as of the 2022 General Convention, two forms of Eucharistic Prayer C as alternatives to the form given in the prayer book. A word about the expansive language liturgies of EOW: the notion of "expansive" language means to go beyond gender "inclusive" language, to expand for our liturgical use the range of the metaphors and images that exist in the canon of the Bible and the tradition. The Episcopal Church's commitment to move toward expansive language is not without resistance from some quarters, but it is a firm commitment. As we saw in Chapter One, this commitment was reinforced at the 2018 General Convention resolution A068 in passing the trial use of an expansive language version of the Rite II Eucharistic liturgy. This adds a charge to the all-important work of clergy and other educators to talk about these new resources and introduce the materials on a steady and intentional basis, with a non-anxious grace. Clergy know well that while education will not change all minds on any issue, minds will rarely be changed without any education at all. But in the end congregations will not become open to our evolving liturgical resources unless they pray with them, since texts for prayer can only been tested by praying. Of course, a congregation can certainly continue to use the 1979 prayer book without any supplementation or amendment, but then they are deprived of a greater deployment of the rich breadth and depth of language that Christians have used of God and the work of God over the centuries. The use of the new resources is, in other words, a spiritual issue in our worship, and the refusal to use them is a missed opportunity in our expression of thanksgiving to God and in our formation.

Musically, the *Hymnal 1982* became our standard resource shortly after the 1979 book was adopted, and musical planning is of course curation from beginning to end! Since that time other hymnals and musical resources have been developed, including *Wonder Love and Praise* (a supplement with many more modern and world folk offerings), *Lift Every Voice* II (indebted to the African American tradition), and *Voices Found* (indebted to women composers and musicians). There is a Spanish language hymnal, *El Himnario*, though many Spanish-speaking congregations prefer a hymnal known as *Flor y Canto*.

In the following pages of this chapter I will work through the Sunday Eucharist and offer selective commentary on the resources to be curated in its planning, *using Rite II as the primary reference*, since it is the form of the Eucharist we know is considered the principal Sunday liturgy by the majority of our parishes and other ecclesial communities.[2] While the curation of music is of great importance, and music is central to the liturgy, one book cannot do everything and, while I am musically literate, there are others more qualified than I to offer such a guide. Because the scope of this book is primarily the curation of texts and scripts and recommendations on their ritual performance, I will thus be focusing on the prayer book and the first volume of EOW, on the BOS 2018[3] to a lesser

---

2. Where there is a significant difference in rubrics of the two rites, I note that fact and comment on it as necessary.

3. The 2018 version of the BOS, with certain amendments, was approved by General Convention in 2022. This is the version to which I will refer throughout.

extent, where its resources come to bear on the Sunday, and on the recent texts put forward by General Convention.

As a matter of organization, the reader should note that there is quite a lot of material to work with here, so I will work through the 1979 prayer book *as it is,* along with its supplementation by BOS and EOW. At certain points within that exposition, I will mention specific changes to Rite II made by the two recent General Conventions, but I will not speak to every single change that simply alters unnecessary gender reference without any other significant liturgical or doctrinal import.

Liturgy of the Word from the Prayer Book and EOW

Let us begin a walk-through of the Sunday rites, and the reader will want to have the *Book of Common Prayer* 1979 and the first volume of EOW close at hand. The Eucharist begins with an **entrance rite** which on a normal Sunday is composed of Acclamation, a Song of Praise (or a hymn that replaces it) and/or the Kyrie, and Collect of the Day that, for a substantial portion of the year is shaped by the lectionary and seasonal calendar of observance. It is theologically significant that we begin the liturgy with acclamation—strictly speaking, a shout or a cry of affirmation that honors the one being acclaimed. All our life begins in God and arises from God, and our redemption and hope as well. Before we petition God for anything, or say another word, we honor God's name. Joined with an opening hymn (usually for procession), this sounds the first note of the Eucharist: our joyous indebtedness to

God's grace. The 1979 book offers three options for an opening Acclamation—one standard and trinitarian in content and
two that correspond to the paschal center of gravity of the
book, i.e., Lent and the Great Fifty Days of Easter. The former
acclaims the one who forgives, and the latter uses the ancient
Easter Greeting with Alleluia. The expansive language version
of Rite II authorized for trial use by General Convention gives
an additional standard Acclamation that replaces the partly
gendered version of the trinitarian formula—"Father, Son,
and Holy Spirit"—with "most holy, glorious, and undivided
Trinity." One could argue from the position that person-like
language is essential to doctrine and thus that this change is
undesirable, but it is hard to argue that the change is theologically problematic as such. And, of course, such a rendering as
the latter gives has also been a part of the history of Christian
worship, and it clearly implies and in no way denies that the
undivided trinity is, in fact, a trinity of (in the creedal sense)
"persons."

EOW I commendably expands the range of Acclamations.
In addition to a general Acclamation that praises the one, holy,
and living God—using language both central to Christian
faith and to the language of Scripture in both Testaments—
and an Acclamation of great simplicity that is also used on
Good Friday, it offers options for Advent and an additional
Acclamation for Lent that expands the metaphoric range of
our praise. The Advent Acclamation draws out the themes
of the coming of Christ and its purpose: to set us free. The
Lenten Acclamation includes the forgiveness of sins on
which the 1979 Acclamation is focused, but also speaks to
God's "bearing our burdens" through Christ. Soteriological

language[4] in the Bible and in the Christian tradition includes metaphors centered on healing, deliverance from bondage into freedom, blessing, empowerment, salvation, unification, illumination, raising up of the spirit, the offering of refuge, the full flourishing of life... and more. Having more than one Lenten Acclamation allows us to tap ever so slightly into more of that range, and we might be well-advised to develop additional options in the ongoing process of liturgical renewal and development.

The Eucharistic entrance can be modified as a Penitential Rite. In the Episcopal Church this is commonly used in Lent, though it can be used at any time in which a penitential tone is appropriate. Several horrifying cases of violence against persons of color in the last several years—cases that have led us again to a national reckoning over our nation's systemic racism— have prompted the use of the Penitential Rite by some ecclesial communities, regardless of the time of the church year. This is a fine example of the wise curation of ritual forms in response to the pressures of cultural context—one of several criteria for liturgical curation that we will consider below. It is also not uncommon for churches to use the Great Litany on page 148 of the prayer book, or in an expansive language form on page 46 of EOW 1, on the first Sunday of Lent to set the penitential tone of the season. Planners should pay particular attention to the directions for grafting the Litany into the Sunday Eucharist.[5] (The Enrollment of Candidates who will

---

4. "Soteriology" concerns the problem of the human situation and the remedy that God brings to it. It does not mean, narrowly, "salvation," though "salvation" is one of the soteriological metaphors.

5. BCP, p. 153.

be baptized at the Great Vigil of Easter is especially appropriate for the First Sunday of Lent, but if one deploys the Great Litany for Lent 1, it is arguably better to defer this Enrollment to the Second Sunday of Lent. This allows the force of both the Great Litany and the Enrollment of Candidates to have their due.) The Supplication following the Great Litany is especially appropriate in times of national emergency or distress, and might be used before the Eucharist on a Sunday if the situation calls for it.

Following the Collect for Purity (required in Rite I, optional in Rite II—see my comments in Chapter Six), the Gloria and/or either the Kyrie or Trisagion are offered, as appropriate to season and subject to the directions on page 406 of the prayer book. (Rite I may include the Kyrie and Gloria, as well as the recitation of the commandments—a commendable modification in the Lenten season or at other penitential times.) The Gloria has a long tradition of use in the Eucharist but can be replaced by another appropriate hymn. Any hymn that is appropriately expressive of praise is possible, but appropriate Canticles, appointed for Morning Prayer, can be used in the Eucharist and they are a good choice as well. That the Canticles can be used for this purpose, including those in EOW, is made explicit in General Convention's resolution 2018-D078 that contains the whole text of the expansive language version of Rite II (see Appendix C). EOW 1 supplements the possible Songs of Praise in two ways: by providing expansive language renderings of the already existent prayer book Canticles 12, 15, 16, 18, and 21, and by providing some beautiful *new* biblical Canticles for use. EOW 1 also provides a handful of Canticles that set into poetic form writings from

Anselm of Canterbury and Julian of Norwich. Whatever one thinks of this new direction of non-biblical Canticles, the new biblical Canticles in EOW (labeled by letter instead of number) are lovely. For alternatives to the Gloria, the following are immediately obvious.

- Canticle C, "The Song of Hannah" (I Samuel 2:1-8), "My heart exults in you, O God..."
- Canticle J, "A Song of Judith" (Judith 16:13-16), "I will sing a new song to my God..."
- Canticle K, "A Song of our Adoption" (Ephesians 1:3-10), "Blessed are you, the God and Father of our Lord Jesus Christ...."
- Canticle M, "A Song of Faith" (I Peter 1: 3-4, 18-21), "Blessed be the God and Father of our Lord Jesus Christ...."

For themes of creation, Canticle 12, "A Song of Creation," and the new Canticle D, "A Song of the Wilderness," are excellent choices. This seems to be one point in the service, as long as it is not a season when the Kyrie or Trisagion are appointed, where a sense of our being a member of an entire created order that hymns the goodness of God is almost always appropriate.

It seems good to make some use of these biblical Canticles provided in EOW, though the one responsible for curating forms will need to reflect on the pattern of their usage along with the Gloria or musical resources from authorized hymnals. They offer an enrichment of biblical language and thereby stretch our vision of that for which we offer our praise to God.

The appropriate Collect of the Day is specified for each Sunday, and in the seasons the planner is beholden to use the designated choice which is tied to themes of the season and day. However, in "ordinary time" (not a term Episcopalians used to use, but which has now been appropriated from the Revised Common Lectionary), the Collects tend toward a more general set of themes not always tied directly to the lectionary. In these periods, some curation of the supplemental Collects on EOW 1 page 51ff. is warranted and this provides an opportunity to pick up creation themes in some of the Canticles or in Scripture.

The **lectionary** is not at the direction of local leaders, except in "Ordinary Time" when a choice must be made between the two tracks. There is ample guidance in other books about the differences between the tracks. EOW provides an alternative form for the proclamation and response to the reading of Scripture that is worthy of consideration: "Hear what the Spirit is saying to God's people," or "Hear what the Spirit is saying to the Churches." These can replace the BCP form, "The Word of the Lord," or "Here ends the reading." The option is included in the expansive language version of Rite II authorized in 2018 (again, Appendix C). At a minimum, the alternative form may be commended as a fresh provocation of the congregation's attention. But one could argue that the new form is a better alternative in some cases, when the Scripture appointed is full of violence or depredation, when it is more than a little jarring to respond to it immediately after as "the Word of the Lord." I am not at all suggesting that the assembly does not hold that Scripture *overall* is breathed of God. Of course, the **Sermon** can and should always address this kind of reading through interpretation and the provision of context where possible, but that does not make certain kinds of violence in the proclamation of the Word any less jarring. We testify to Scripture as the Word of the Lord because it testifies in turn, ultimately, to the Living Word that is Christ. But Episcopalians (Anglicans in general) are neither literalists nor "bibliolatrists." Taking Scripture with high seriousness does not lead us to declare that everything in Scripture is necessary to salvation, only that all things necessary to salvation are within Scripture.[6] With this in mind, the alternative "Hear what the Spirit is saying to the Churches" strikes the perfect pitch; it acknowledges that God speaks to us through Scripture but avoids identifying the Word of God with every single line or word of the text. The EOW alternative itself reflects the rhetoric of the second chapter of the Revelation to John, thus being itself thoroughly biblical.

The next significant fixed element in the liturgy after the Sermon is the **Creed.** The decision here is fairly straightforward: to use the Nicene Creed as provided in the prayer book or as provided in EOW 1. Until our recent changes, it has been rubrically required that the Nicene Creed be used on Sundays and Major Feasts and, while there are some concerns about the Nicene Creed's use, whether or not well-informed, it is a text of great ecumenical significance. There are other churches that have authorized a repertoire of creedal responses to the proclamation of the Word (e.g., the Presbyterian Church USA) and those options are the result of long and careful church-wide discernment by those who offer them. The significance of the Nicene Creed to ecumenical theology and Anglican ecclesiology suggests that we should enter into the same careful discernment before offering alternatives to it. The use, with

---

6. See point one of the Chicago-Lambeth Quadrilateral, BCP, p. 877.

the bishop's permission, of the Order for Celebrating the Holy Eucharist as the principal liturgy of the day, which is now allowed, could make for the use of some other creed, but this is a significant change for Episcopalians that deserves prayerful thought before we make it.

So, what of the alternatives we now have for the Nicene Creed, which most of us will likely stick with, whether 1979 prayer book or EOW 1? What do we take into account in making our decisions about use?

Let us begin by recalling that whenever we use in worship the hymns, creeds, or other theological symbols written originally in another language, we are working in translation, and translation is not a math exercise; it is interpretive. We all do well to temper our positions on such liturgical forms with a good dose of humility. With that in mind, let us consider the three notable features of the Nicene Creed in the EOW text that differ from the 1979 book, two of which seem to inspire the most excitement or, alternatively, reluctance, about them. *As long as these two remain options,* then the curator of liturgical forms is likely to make a decision on the basis of their own position or the congregation's position on theology, gender-bias, or our ecumenical responsibilities.

The change least subject to controversy seems to be the grammatical alteration in the third stanza of the Creed—that concerning the Holy Spirit. The lines concerning the Spirit's source and work—"who proceeds... who with the Father and the Son... who has spoken..."—are rendered as dependent clauses, which eliminates the need for a gendered reference to the Spirit as we have in the 1979 book, without making any real theological change. It also, by the way, returns this stanza to the grammatical form (though not the Tudor idiom) that we used in the 1928 book, by which the gendering of the Spirit was avoided. It honors the principle in expansive language practice in which gendering is not used at all where it is not necessary to theological substance or meaning and makes no change to either.

The second change, more controversial for some, also lies in the third stanza: the removal of the *filioque*. In the 1979 book, a form of the Creed that western rite churches have long used indicates that the Spirit proceeds from the Father *and the Son*. This is the *filioque* clause, and students of theology will immediately recognize how fraught this clause can be. In the original form of the Nicene Creed, the Spirit is actually confessed to proceed *from the Father*. To dig deeply into the complexities of this shift to the *filioque* is a larger task than this book can accomplish in size or scope. Suffice to say here that the change was in part theological, in part linguistic, and in part an effect of erroneous assumptions. Theologically, western rite Christians have emphasized in their thinking about the Trinity Augustine's powerful image of the Spirit as the bond of love between the Father and the Son. Eastern rite Christians, while not rejecting this biblically grounded view, have considered the twofold procession of the Spirit in western theology to undermine the preeminence of the first person as the *source* of the Trinity's life. Furthermore, for our eastern Christian siblings, the change made by westerners to the original form of the creed has been a longstanding sore point, taken to be an insult to our ecumenical heritage and a departure from the ancient faith. Linguistically, the argument has been complicated by the differences in the Greek and

Latin, with the original term in Greek (*ekporeumai*) connoting origin, and the translated term in Latin (*procedere*) connoting movement which might or might not imply origin. In terms of erroneous—and fateful!—assumptions, it seems that the earliest insertion of the *filioque* in Toledo was accompanied by an assumption on the part of the bishops that the *filioque* was in the original creed as it was ratified at Constantinople in 381. It was not.

Anecdotally, I would say that the omission of the *filioque* is the most controversial change in the EOW form of the Creed. But we must note that the Episcopal Church has joined a wider ecumenical groundswell in the west to move back to the use of the original Creed that had no *filioque*. Lambeth called all churches in communion with Canterbury to consider this change as early as 1978; the World Council of Churches echoed this in 1987; and the General Convention of the Episcopal Church in 1994 resolved that the *filioque* would be removed from the Creed with the printing of the next prayer book. Other Anglican churches, and even the Roman Catholic church, have been moving steadily in this direction. Reflecting this commitment, the earlier versions of the first volume of EOW 1 had the *filioque* bracketed; the current version removes it entirely. The 1994 resolution was complicated by the fact that we did not move toward a new prayer book within the time frame that was envisioned in 1994, but *it is finally the Nicene Creed as reformulated in EOW I that now appears in the 2018 expansive language revision of Rite II*. The decision could, in theory, be reversed, but it seems unlikely. Given the indicators, it would be wise for liturgical leaders to educate their congregations about this issue and give them the opportunity, at least from time to time, to pray the EOW rendering of the Nicene Creed. Praying alternative texts, combined with patient and gracious education, is the only way that controverted liturgical changes can be detoxified.

There is one remaining change in the EOW Creed, and that is in the second clause, concerning the Son. In place of the 1979 rendering—"...by the power of the Holy Spirit, he became incarnate from the Virgin Mary, and was made man"—in the EOW version we have "...was incarnate of the Holy Spirit and the Virgin Mary and became truly human." The grammatical shift is in line, again, with the general principle of expansive language that where gender references are not needed or, in the case of the Bible, are not in the text, we don't use them. The shift from "man" to "human" reflects the fact that what is soteriologically significant about Jesus Christ is not that he was a man, but that he was human. (He certainly did not come to take on only the nature of males!) The language of cooperation between the Holy Spirit and the Virgin Mary takes very seriously the role of Mary as *Theotokos*, whose "yes" made possible the Incarnation, and whose partnership with the Holy Spirit neatly reflects the doctrine that both the fullness of God and the fullness of humanity is present in Christ. In my experience, those who are troubled by the changes in the second clause of the Creed are troubled by this particular wording and will occasionally hold forth about how it is a departure from "ancient doctrine." But, in fact, this particular grammatical construction is as old as the so-called *Apostolic Tradition*, a document dating in its earliest layers from around 215 CE, and in its latest from perhaps the mid-4th century. Occasionally, we get tangled up in our assumptions that the recent way in which we have phrased something is somehow blessed with the patina of ancient dogma, when this is not actually the case. The language of the EOW Creed on this point is as old, or older, than that of the 1979 book's version.

The next section of the liturgy continues the people's response to the Word of God. Having felt ourselves rise together after the Sermon and join in voicing the Creed as one, we now turn to our Intercessions for the world, called in the prayer book the "Prayers of the People." The prayer book specifies those matters to which our Intercessions should turn and provides six forms for doing so. The church in the 1970s was just learning to intercede in this way, having been accustomed to the "Prayer for the Whole State of Christ's Church" that survives in Rite I of the 1979 book which, in the 1928 book, was to be read by the priest. The six forms on pages 383 to 395 of the 1979 prayer book, though never required, were a good way to learn how to offer intercessions. They are now best retired. This is a point in the liturgy where familiarity can become anesthetic, and cease to evoke the engagement of the assembly. The needs of the world are fresh every week, and so should be our prayers for that world. Church Publishing offers resources for weekly intercessions in *Planning for Rites and Rituals: A Resource for Episcopal Worship.*[7] There is much to learn from our communion partners, the Evangelical Lutheran Church, about how to offer evocative and creative Intercessions: *Sundays and Seasons* is the web-based resource of the Evangelical Lutheran Church in America and is well worth a subscription in addition to Rite Planning, an Episcopal

---

7. https://www.churchpublishing.org/planningforritesandrituals

online resource. Liturgical leaders may curate these forms, or adapt them, or create their own. A good way to develop the practice of intercession is to create a guild composed of those who have talents at composition, and can compose prayers that resonate with the themes of the lections or the season. The most important task here is to write Intercessions that are not simply a recitation by the Intercessor, but a moving provocation to the assembly to *pray.*

We have four forms now for the **Confession of Sin,** the final act of response in the Liturgy of the Word—although, the entire Liturgy of the Table is in its own way a response to the Word as well, an eating of the Word under the signs of bread and wine, like Ezekiel who swallowed the scroll.[8] The Confession in the 1979 prayer book will be familiar to Episcopalians in its acknowledgement of "what we have done and what we have left undone." This longstanding rhetorical turn in Anglican forms for Confession is brilliant in its simultaneous compression and comprehension, its linkage of our sins of commission and omission to the command to love, and a petition for the delight in that command and the will to follow it. The alternative Confession in EOW 1 sounds the same notes overall, but foregrounds sin as the denial of the goodness with which God has created us. Some might say that a reminder of the basic goodness of creation is a welcome antidote to notions of wrongdoing that make of humanity something fundamentally unworthy. The EOW Confession of Sin is to be commended for yet another broadening of soteriological imagery (forgiveness, restoration, strengthening), and

---

8. Ezekiel 3:3.

it broadens our accountability for the wider patterns of evil in which we find ourselves complicit, closely connecting this confession to the breadth of the Baptismal renunciations of sin at the personal, social, and cosmic level.[9]

Other Supplements to the Liturgy of the Word

Before proceeding to the Peace and to a close assessment of the options we curate for the Liturgy of the Table, we should consider other liturgical forms that might come to bear on the assembly's Sunday celebration either at the beginning of the liturgy, before or after the Creed, or after the Prayers (and Confession)—specifically, forms provided in the *Book of Occasional Services*.

There are options for the beginning of the liturgy in "The Church Year" section of the BOS. It has become more common than ever for Episcopal ecclesial communities to have a formal lighting of an **Advent Wreath** to help mark the Sundays of that season, and equally common to involve the children of a parish in the lighting. It is incumbent on us to note that the BOS does not provide for this, reflecting the same concern that it manifests for the placement of the Advent wreath itself in its rubrics: neither its placement nor the lighting should interfere with the central symbols or actions of the community—Font and Book and Table.[10] Rather, the BOS prefers the lighting of the Advent Wreath on the Lord's Day occur at the same time as the lighting of other candles in preparation for worship to begin. For those who choose creatively to "break" the rubric

---

9. BCP, p. 302.
10. BOS 2018, p. 20.

and have a special lighting and prayers, it is wise to take to take this concern seriously. The Advent Wreath lighting ought to be a brief and simple affair, with a preparatory tone, and not overshadow Word or Sacrament.

The BOS also provides for the longstanding Anglican tradition of **Lessons and Carols**. The rubrics rightly suggest that this service be separate from the Sunday Eucharist—on a Sunday evening, for example—because this ritual has its own special, self-contained rhythm and movement. Those who curate our liturgical forms might better preserve its beauty and power by letting it stand alone. Still, some will choose to allow Lessons and Carols to serve as the Liturgy of the Word for the Sunday Eucharist sometime in Advent and/or Christmas. Certainly it should not be done more than once, for the sake of the basic rhythm of the season, and one of the curator's questions will be *when* to use it. Having it either initiate the Advent season or conclude it is one common choice; another is, at Christmas, to have it the first (or second, when there falls a second) Sunday after. If Lessons and Carols *is* to be observed as the Sunday liturgy of the Word, a Sermon must be preached.

From time to time, the Feast of the Presentation (February 2) will fall on a Sunday, and this Major Feast is one of only three, the others being The Holy Name (January 1) and the Transfiguration (August 6), that take precedence over the Sunday *when they fall on the Sunday*. These are days when the presence of Christ's name in all that exists, and the work of God not to abolish flesh but to transform it, provides some connection to the celebration of creation. There is a long-standing tradition of a **Candlemas** procession that plays on the theme of light that is so prominent in the Incarnation cycle, especially so in the season after Epiphany, and the BOS provides a ritual for this procession beginning on page 42.

There are many other ritual resources in the BOS section on "The Church Year" that are not intended for use on Sunday. Several commendable examples expand the cultural rituals appropriate to a diverse church, particularly as our Spanish and French speaking membership continues to grow.[11] (The charge by recent meetings of the General Convention to create good, dynamic translations of all these resources is a most important task, and overdue.) These I will not comment on since most do not pertain to Sunday liturgies, but they are rich resources and liturgical planners who serve diverse communities should take appreciative note of them. I do wish to comment on two additional resources in the BOS—one that sometimes is folded into the Sunday liturgy and shouldn't be, and the other, though it does not occur as part of the Eucharist, but which *can* occur on a Sunday. Both are worthy of attention as well because of the moment in which we find ourselves with respect to the peril of the creation of which we are charged to be stewards.

The first of these is **St. Francis Day**. This Lesser Feast[12] *does not take precedence over the Eucharist of the Lord's Day*, and when the calendar rubrics are broken on this point,[13] the fuss around animal blessings, animals in church, or Francis himself, often end up overshadowing the central themes and symbols of the Lord's Day. Nothing should trump the paschal nexus

---

11. BOS 2018, pp. 25-31; 115-116; 249-278.
12. LFF 2006, p. 405.
13. BCP, p. 15-16.

of Baptism and Eucharist on the Lord's Day and its focus on Christ. As an aside, even where done correctly (i.e., not supplanting the Lord's Day Eucharist), it is not unknown to see Francis observed for his love of creation with little attention given to other salient facts of his life—his radical commitment to the gospel for which he left family behind, his radical poverty and its implications for a world awash in consumer values, and his interreligious openness, all of which has contributed to his impact as a beloved figure around the world and across religions. Yet, in a world amid a climate crisis as a result at least in part of poor human stewardship of the earth, Francis's commitment to creation may indeed be important to hold up. Still, it is ideal to keep to the rubrics and make the Francis celebration *separate from* and perhaps immediately following the Sunday Eucharist. I have seen this quite successfully done and, in this format, it can be a powerful evangelistic opportunity for the local community. Let the reader note that the ritual provided for this observance, with a blessing of animals, is presented in the BOS (page 100ff.) as a *stand-alone rite.*

The other ritual that does not traditionally occur on a Sunday but can, is a **Rogation** procession. There was a time in the Episcopal Church when Rogation days were regularly observed. The Rogation Day's focus on land, food, and harvest, also enacts a respect for creation all too appropriate at this moment of climate crisis. This may well argue for the rogation ritual provided by the BOS on p. 88 to be used more often as we call to mind the church's commitment to creation's stewardship.

The decisions about these sorts of observances are stand-out examples of the sort of things that curators of liturgical forms will need to consider in their planning—more on the criteria for discernment in the next chapter.

There is a second major section of the BOS, following material tied to the calendar, called "Pastoral Services." A number of these are forms that can be curated for Sundays when relevant.

The most important of these rituals, rooted deeply in Baptism and at the heart of the paschal theology of the 1979 book, are forms for the process for the adult **Catechumenate**. Inspired by the Roman Catholic RCIA and adapted over time, these forms provide an opportunity for admission to a period of preparation by adults who are moving from inquiry into the faith into its deeper exploration, forms for the congregation to enter into prayer for the Catechumens as they explore, and enrollment to Candidacy for Baptism for those whose exploration leads them to the threshold of formal commitment to the Christian life. Beyond the work that clergy and catechists do with the Catechumens, the BOS rites and prayers make it possible for the whole congregation to support them in their preparation through formal prayer. Those who have implemented the Catechumenate over the years will know how powerful an impact this process has for the whole congregation's formation. Having adults in their midst who are preparing seriously for Baptism typically prompts the rest of the assembly to revisit their own Baptismal vows. Parallel resources are now available in the BOS for the preparation of parents and sponsors of children being baptized, and for those who are preparing to renew their Baptismal commitment in Confirmation, Reception, and Reaffirmation. All these can be found on pages 125ff. in the "Pastoral Services" section of the BOS 2018.

Prayers for persons over the course of their candidacy obviously take place publicly during the Prayers of the People, so the rites for Admission and Enrollment are rubrically indicated for a position either before or after the Creed. Curators of liturgy will in planning need to decide which place is best, and there is something to be said for either position. Placing the rite before the Creed allows the Sermon to address what is immediately about to occur, and then the whole assembly moves after the Catechumenal rite directly into the confession of faith together, a powerful conclusion to the Admission or Enrollment; on the other hand, placing the rite after the Creed moves neatly into the prayers for the Catechumens/Candidates, and may flow a little more smoothly, ritually speaking. In either case, any church that is preparing adults for Baptism that fails to take advantage of these liturgical forms misses an opportunity both for the full liturgical expression of our trust in God and the formation that results from that expression.

In addition to the rich Catechumenal resources, there are in the "Pastoral Services" section of the BOS[14] a range of other short rites and, in some cases, directions or suggestions for ritualization that can occur in the context of the Sunday liturgy. These include the **welcoming and sending** of members of the congregation, recognition of **particular ministries** by baptized members and commissionings for them, the **anniversary of a marriage**, a commemoration of **retirement,** and many more, including, in the BOS 2022 version, a ritual for **renaming**. The

---

14. BOS, pp. 117ff.

reader is encouraged to peruse these, paying close attention to the rubrics. Most of these are appropriately conducted at the time just before the Peace, which allows for the latter action to conclude the ritual by placing the center of gravity back on the whole assembly as it moves into the liturgy of the Table.

Liturgy of the Table from the Prayer Book and EOW

After the Peace, we move toward the celebration of the Sacrament. Here we turn to one of the most important acts of curation that the planner will undertake: which **Eucharistic Prayer** to use? Short of Scripture itself, the Eucharistic Prayer is the longest and certainly the most theologically dense, fixed element of the assembly's worship in the entire liturgy.

Most clergy have been working with the four alternatives in Rite II for decades now, and very few clergy remain who know the 1928 *Book of Common Prayer*, in practice. Still, it is important to linger over the Eucharistic Prayers at some length, if for no other reason because many communities in the Episcopal Church are familiar with all those possible forms in the prayer book, yet seem to use Eucharistic Prayer A almost exclusively! To miss the opportunity to use the whole range of Eucharistic Prayers in the 1979 book—beautifully augmented by three new ones in EOW 1—is to miss some of the richness available for our communal prayer. I will therefore spend what might seem disproportionate time on a review of these prayers for the curator, but, as I noted above, there is no other single place in the liturgy save Scripture itself where so much theology is proclaimed, and so comprehensively in its form. (There are those who have dismissed the new EOW Eucharistic Prayers rather quickly but, in my view, without much informed analysis. Certainly there are a couple of points at which these prayers can be improved, but that is equally true of the 1979 prayers, and on a couple of points that I will address below, the EOW prayers could be considered superior to the BCP options.) A note on what follows: a fine summary of the history of our Eucharistic Prayers can be found in Marion Hatchett's still serviceable *Commentary on the American Prayer Book*.[15] Readers interested in a *systematic* history of the prayers and their gradual amendment should look to Hatchett, as I touch history lightly here only as it goes directly to theology and bears on curation.

Let us interject some attention to Rite I and then return to Rite II, but before we do so, let me note some changes made by General Convention that touch on *all* the Eucharistic Prayers.

First, in place of **"The Lord be with you"** we may use "God be with you." This change is hardly a theological "ditch to die in," but some will find it a welcome change. To say "God be with you" does not deny that God is the Lord (one with authority), while it sidesteps the masculine association that the term "Lord" has in history. For others, our distance from the middle ages combined with the de-facto use of the term Lord simply to mean God, and its use simply to signify God's oversight of creation with no particular masculine association, will make this change seem superfluous. There is also some connotative association of the term "God be with you" as a message to those in trouble, or as a kind of "adieu" offered at a

---

15. Marion J. Hatchett, *Commentary on the American Prayer Book* (New York: HarperOne, 1995).

parting, and time will tell whether it can do the same linguistic work of "The Lord be with you" within the Eucharistic rite.

Another change in the expansive language Rite II is the possibility of changing the **Benedictus** (concluding the **Sanctus**) using "Blessed is the One who comes in the name of the Lord" as well as the given form, "Blessed is he who comes...." This is arguably another example of an expansive language change in which something is accomplished while nothing is really lost. Notwithstanding the common though not universal practice of members of the assembly crossing themselves at the Benedictus, the reference to "he" or "the one who comes" is to Christ. It is taken from the Lukan narrative of the entry of Jesus into Jerusalem (with Psalm 118 behind it), so that the Sanctus and Benedictus connect the holiness and transcendence of God in Isaiah 6 ("Holy, Holy, Holy") to the immanence of God coming to die in Jerusalem as servant of all. Yet, there is some truth hidden in the impulse some have to cross themselves at the Benedictus; though it refers to Christ, we are in this liturgy about to eat the bread of the Lord as the Body of Christ, so that we too, in fact, come in the name of the Lord. The multivalent phrase "Blessed is the One who comes in the name of the Lord" preserves that meaning while losing nothing of its reference to Christ as well.

Eucharistic Prayers of Rite I

The two **Eucharistic Prayers of Rite I**[16] are the direct descendants in both theology and idiom of the prayers of Thomas Cranmer. Prayer I is the closest to its predecessors, with Prayer

---

16. BCP, beginning on p. 333.

II amending what can be taken to be shortcomings of Prayer I in our present context. Both of these prayers offer the narrow and very tight linkage between the *sacrifice/offering* of Christ and his *death* which, soteriologically, holds center stage. Prayer II offers a slight nod in the direction of the wider scope of the Incarnation ("to take our nature upon him") and also corrects the absence of any reference to creation—understandable for a time in which Communion might have been appended to Morning Prayer, but still a shortcoming by the measure of both early and classical Eucharistic Prayers and our present context. Both prayers I and II sound strong notes of the Eucharist as memorial, and both sound the benefits of Communion not only as the forgiveness of sins (by the grace of God, not by the power of the Eucharist), but as a *participation* in Christ in the eating of the meal, consistent with settled aspects of Anglican Eucharistic theology since Richard Hooker. Neither prayer has an epiclesis (an invocation of the Holy Spirit) over the assembly, strictly speaking, but simply asks that the assembly be "filled with [God's] grace and heavenly benediction," restricting the invocation of the Spirit to the gifts of bread and wine. In this, these two prayers follow the pattern of the western rite and of Cranmer's 1549 Eucharistic Prayer.

When curating among the Eucharistic Prayers of the 1979 book, it is permissible to use the **Prayers of Rite II in Rite I**, simply by rendering the formal vernacular of Rite II into the Tudor idiom.[17] This is not an option to which Rite I communities often opt (and in my experience, not one of which many are even aware), but it is a missed opportunity, because the

---

17. BCP, p.14.

Prayers of Rite II draw on other soteriological and pneumato-
logical traditions of Eucharistic praying, and their use would
provide communities that prefer Rite I a more robust spiritual
and theological *range* for thanksgiving and prayer, richer with
additional biblical imagery.

Eucharistic Prayers of Rite II

In Rite II, **Eucharistic Prayer A**[18] is intended to convey in the
formal vernacular the core of the Cranmerian theology present
in the first prayer of Rite I, while riffing on the corrections
that Prayer II provides. (One should note, however, that Rite
I Prayer II offers thanks more prominently for creation itself,
and our being made in that context; Rite II Prayer A is more
anthropocentric, with a focus on *our* being created by God
for relationship with God.) Prayer A expands the reference
to the Incarnation beyond the focus on sin alone—"to share
our human nature, to live and die as one of us"—and then
turns to the metaphor of reconciliation as the purpose of the
Incarnation. Further specifying the nature of that reconciliation, the next clause turns to the death of Christ on the cross
as a "perfect sacrifice for the whole world," thus extending the
Cranmerian identification of Christ's sacrifice as, specifically,
his *death*.

Following the Words of Institution that our prayers univer-
sally include, there is then a summary acclamation and a focus,
again, on "memorial." Here, Prayer A goes farther than
the Cranmerian lineage, even from 1549, and restores from
earlier euchological models a robust and direct invocation of

---

18. BCP, p. 361ff.

the Holy Spirit (epiclesis) over both the gifts of bread and wine and over the assembly, with the gifts being for the assembly's strengthening for service. The inclusion of a robust epiclesis is one of the several ways in which, as Massey Shepherd purportedly said, "each revision of the prayer book has taken us one step toward the East." We do well to remember that Christianity, though often taught as a "western religion" now, was born in the middle east, and the sources of our prayer are African, Syrian, and Palestinian in their origins, most all of which have a strong epiclesis, though not always in the same place. The epiclesis dropped out of the western tradition, preoccupied as it was with a theology of the sacrament focused on Christ and his Words from the synoptic gospels, and rather famously inattentive to matters of pneumatology. All contemporary Eucharistic Prayers of the Episcopal Church include a clear epiclesis with one exception (Prayer C),[19] and increasingly (in later prayers) manifest a strong trinitarian structure. This is not uniquely Episcopalian, or Anglican; it reflects a growing ecumenical consensus on the structure and content of newer compositions of the Eucharistic Prayer.

With respect to planning, no single Eucharistic Prayer is appropriate or inappropriate for any particular season or feast. However, for those curating the Prayers on the basis of their theological themes, Prayer A is perhaps best used during penitential seasons. Lent is an obvious candidate; Advent might be as well, though the linkage of Advent to Christmas and Epiphany in an Incarnation cycle leads many to

---

19. This has been corrected in the trial versions of Prayer C, discussed below.

choose a single prayer for that period, with more emphasis on incarnational themes. The expansive language Rite II Prayer A does increase ever so slightly the attention to creation, as a companion to Incarnation, by replacing "reconcile us to you, the God and Father of all," with "reconcile us to you, the God and maker of all. In this way the new version does some of the same work as Rite I Prayer II did for Prayer I, bringing creation slightly more into the foreground of the assembly's consciousness.

The seed of **Eucharistic Prayer B**[20] is one of the prayers from a document known as the *Apostolic Tradition*, which has exercised great influence on the Anglican tradition, largely though not solely through the influence of Gregory Dix. The *Apostolic Tradition* was taken to be very old—early 3rd century—and was thought possibly to be Roman, though we have since learned that it is more likely West Syrian in origin, and may date from a somewhat later moment. Even so, in my estimation it is no older than the 4th century, and certain elements of it reflect an extremely early Christology, so it is a *layered* prayer. The importance of this prayer at the time of the modern liturgical movement meant *de facto* that it would become a model for many modern Anglican prayers. In fact, nearly every province of the Anglican Communion has at least a supplemental Eucharistic Prayer that is shaped by the *Apostolic Tradition*.[21]

Prayer B begins with a doxological narrative of salvation

---

20. BCP, p. 367ff.

21. The reader is encouraged simply to scan through the Anglican Eucharistic prayers presented by Colin Buchanan, *Anglican Eucharistic Liturgies 1985-2010: The Authorized Rites of the Anglican Communion* (Norwich: Canterbury Press, 2011).

history weaving the creation together with the role of the people of Israel (unlike Prayer A), and moving into an emphasis on Incarnational language, naming Mary, and opening up to a section of great soteriological range: in Christ we are saved, redeemed, delivered from evil, reckoned righteous, brought into truth, and brought from death to life. This already makes this prayer, with its ancient parallels in a tradition of multiple soteriological metaphors, at once a very modern prayer. After the Institution Words and a strong eschatological memorial acclamation, the prayer then offers the ancient and Scriptural "sacrifice of praise and thanksgiving," and offers the bread and wine. Next comes a clear epiclesis over the bread and wine, that they may be the sacrament of Christ and his covenant, and then immediately an epiclesis for the assembly's sanctification rendered as a subordinate clause. The expansive language version of Prayer B slightly alters the epiclesis over the assembly. Instead of—"Unite us to your Son in his sacrifice, that we may be acceptable to him, being sanctified by the Holy Spirit…."—we have the following—"Unite us in the sacrifice of Christ, through whom we are made acceptable to you, being sanctified by the Holy Spirit."

This change will be problematic for some. The first clause is changed so as to avoid the masculine reference ("Son"), but as it falls on the ear it seems to unite the assembly in Christ's sacrifice rather than uniting the assembly to Christ by way of his sacrifice. It is, in short, less relational, though it does push to the foreground that we enter into his sacrifice as a matter of discipleship. "Through whom we are made acceptable to you" is, if the prayer is to maintain its use of a dependent clause, arguably a better expression of faith that God does in fact accept us, by his promise, but it does lose some active force the epiclesis had in the prayer in its earliest form. This is one we will need to pray with for a bit, to test its theology and its piety.

The Prayer closes with an eschatological vision of the dominion of Christ at the end of time, at which we will enter the fullness of the life he has prepared for us.

With its attention to Mary and the Incarnation, as well as its eschatological vision, Prayer B is often used for some or all of the Incarnation cycle. It is wise to remember that the season after Epiphany (which maintains some of its themes early on) is rather long, whereas Advent and Christmas seasons together are shorter; therefore one can certainly make an argument for using one prayer at least for Advent and Christmas and maybe into the Second Sunday after Epiphany. (Recall how important familiarity and repetition are to ritualization, as we saw in Chapter Two, and how change in forms that is too rapid inhibits the community's chance to be formed over time into the vision and vocabulary of a prayer.) Increasingly though, with various streams of modern and contemporary theology opening up the Christian soteriological imagination, Prayer B turns out to be a reasonable choice for the "default" prayer during the long stretches of Ordinary time, and other options from EOW 1 work almost as well in the Incarnation cycle too.

Eucharistic Prayer C[22] has long been the subject of controversy, and so before considering its theology and possible use, we have to acknowledge this controversy. In fact, Episcopalians

---

22. BCP, p. 369ff.

have made something of a sport of criticizing the prayer and even those who find it moving will also identify its shortcomings. Prayer C manifests a different shape than the classical West Syrian shape of our other Eucharistic Prayers—the West Syrian being a powerful narrative form that we inherited from as early as the third century of Christian prayer, bequeathed to us through the Scots. Prayer C is an attempt to reflect our modern scientific knowledge of the universe, though it now seems dated to some. In truth, scientific discovery moves so fast that a prayer written in the Apollo years seemed somewhat dated at its adoption. Before raising questions about it, though, let us honor its positive qualities. Its attempt to reflect the development of our knowledge and our place within a universe far more vast than our capacity to imagine, deserves some credit. Its foregrounding of creation is obviously very important in our present moment and consistent with the chief concerns for liturgical development in the Episcopal Church. The first line of its third stanza—"From the primal elements you brought forth the human race..."—wisely admits of a range of scientific theories of human origins while making doxological language captive to none of them. Its dialogical quality especially commends it, and we might do well to take this as a model for at least some of the Eucharistic Prayers we craft going forward. I have also heard one person after another in my courses over the years tell me how important to their own lives is the phrase: "Deliver us from coming to this table for solace only, and not for strength; for pardon only, and not for renewal." (I once had a student tell me that this line brought her into the Episcopal Church.) The petition here is of course familiar from the history of Anglican Eucharistic Prayers. The prayer's linkage at its climax between the Communion we are about to receive and the revelation of Christ to the disciples at Emmaus is sheer poetry.

The shortcomings of Prayer C are well-rehearsed, even if not always well informed and certainly not conclusive. Among the more peculiar criticisms, the Roman-Alexandrian shape of the prayer (where an epiclesis over the gifts precedes the Words of Institution) raises questions for some about whether the very Body and Blood of Christ are being re-offered to God in the Eucharist. But this criticism assumes an Eastern understanding of the epiclesis that the model of the prayer by definition does not assume, combined with a rather literalistic way of thinking about where the bread and wine "become" the body and Blood of the Lord that has not been the Anglican approach. This Roman-Alexandrian model was the shape of Cranmer's prayer in 1549, suggesting that this peculiar argument is something of a red herring thrown by critics of Prayer C. Certainly, that we have been "made…the rulers of creation" sounds quite off-key in light of our *de facto* confusion of our dominion over the creation with *domination* of it—the effects of which we are now beginning to feel to troubling degree. (Compare the language of Prayer D: "that we might rule *and serve* all your creatures.")[23] One can hardly criticize the drafters of the Prayer for an understanding we have developed since, but it certainly needs to be modified in our current context. Some criticize the address of "Lord God of our Fathers: God of Abraham, Isaac, and Jacob…." and will even now as a kind of conscientious

---

23. BCP, p. 373; emphasis my own.

objection to the prayer, break with it and add the names of
Sarah, Rebekah, Leah, Rachel and other women. I personally
have some sympathy with that and confess to having done
so myself; and yet, there is a deep respect for the tradition
of Israel present in this prayer. The reference to Abraham,
Isaac, and Jacob is formulaic in Judaism, and changing it
may step away from implicit patriarchalism only to step into
a tacit supersessionism. On the other hand, is the use of the
original formula itself regrettably appropriative? The prayer
contains no epiclesis over the assembly, strictly speaking—its
reference to making us "one spirit in Christ" is an effect of
the grace of the sacrament—so if we think an epiclesis over
the assembly is an essential element of Eucharist, the prayer
is lacking in this regard.

One can see, then, that Prayer C has controversial inclu-
sions, though a balanced assessment of it is perhaps incon-
clusive. I have already noted its modernist language, and the
dialogical structure of the prayer begs for its use from time
to time as a performed reminder that the great prayer offered
at Table by the presider is *always* offered on behalf of all. It
is good that all present offer a bit more of the prayer, even
if that need not be a fast rule for all Eucharistic Prayers. Its
theology foregrounds the goodness of the whole creation and
sets us as a people in the context of a vast world, along with
the faithful who have gone before us, declaring the glory
of God. Soteriologically, the prayer offers a strong sense
of sin as betrayal, a breach of trust and relationship. God's
remedy through Christ is to make us "a new people by water
and the Spirit," forging a strong connection to our Baptism.

Communion then both consoles us and strengthens us for
Baptismal service, and makes us one.

There is much to commend this Prayer for use in a penitential season. Its strong sense of sin as a function of human agency
and as the primary purpose of the Incarnation works well there.
In recent years, the environmental crisis has certainly made the
Prayer more apt, even with its shortcomings, although suggestions that we use the Prayer in the northern hemisphere's Fall in
connection with a "creation season" asks the Prayer to do more
than it can (and the proposal to make a "creation season" may itself
misunderstand the purpose of the church's calendar, which always
points to some dimension of Christ's identity and salvific work).

General Convention has worked on this prayer over its last
two meetings. When a full expansive language version of Rite
II was passed in 2018, Prayer C was pulled out, due to concerns
about it that included some of those I enumerated above. The
2022 General Convention has given us a revision of this Prayer
in two different forms: one of them in dialogical form like the
one in the 1979 book, and one with more fixed forms for the
people's responses that nevertheless retain a place for the assembly's voice in its praying.

The two new forms can be seen in Appendix B of this book.
Notable changes in the prayer include the following.

- "Ruler of the Universe" becomes "Source and Sustainer of
  the Universe."
- "Shining light and enfolding dark" is added to the second
  stanza of the pre-Sanctus.
- "Rulers of creation" becomes "stewards of creation."
- "Born of a woman" becomes "born of your servant Mary."

- "To open for us the way…" becomes "opening for us the way…."
- The epiclesis over the bread and wine prior to the institution words is removed.
- Following the anamnesis and oblation there is an epiclesis over the gifts.
- Appended to "let the grace of this Holy Communion" is an epiclesis over the assembly.
- An eschatological petition is added at the end of the Prayer that is at once attentive to the destiny of creation and to the demands of justice and peace.
- Throughout the Prayer, male pronouns that are unnecessary and which can be changed with no clarity of meaning lost are replaced.

These changes seem to me sound. Richer creation imagery, deeper reverence for the significance of Mary, an increase in the language of service and stewardship, and the construction of an epiclesis in the West Syrian placement, as in our other Eucharistic Prayers, are theologically commendable changes and they are, in my view, rhetorically elegant. The eschatological addition at the end of the prayer connects creation with soteriology and eschatology in a way familiar to those who pray with EOW's Eucharistic Prayers. But, again, prayers are *tested* by praying them, and it remains to us to see how it prays.

There is one more change, quite significant, made to the language of the patriarchs referred to above. In place of the 1979 rendering –

"Lord God of our Fathers:

God of Abraham, Isaac and Jacob;
God and Father of Our Lord Jesus Christ' –

we now have –

God of our ancestors;
Redeemer and Mother of Israel;
God and Father of our Lord Jesus Christ....

This change grants an even higher place to the significance of Israel, avoiding in a single stroke both supersessionism and appropriation, lifts up maternal imagery for Israel, gathers in all our ancestors of whatever gender, and maintains the settled language of God as Father.

On the whole, I consider this an excellent contribution to the revision of Prayer C and would suggest that whenever Prayer C is curated for use, that this newer form be used. It will be important to gather the feedback of those assemblies that use it and communicate that to the bishop.

Eucharistic Prayer D[24] is our version of an internationally produced ecumenical text based on the Egyptian anaphora of Basil, a 4th century prayer and one of the most expansive and elegant of Eucharistic Prayers, both in its original form and in its modern renderings. There are parallels in the prayer books of other Christian communions and of several Anglican provinces. Prayer D begins with an extended glorification of God in the context of creation and takes quite some time to move from God's glory, radiance, and goodness to the fracture that occurs—very different from the comparatively quick move to sinfulness made in the Rite I Eucharistic Prayers and

---

24. BCP, p. 372ff.

in Rite II Prayer A. Sin is presented classically as disobedi-ence but is immediately linked to death's power over us. It sounds the persistence of God's call to us, culminating in the Incarnation which brought, not simply forgiveness, but remedy to the poor, to prisoners, to the sorrowful. This is an even more robust acknowledgement of all the purposes of the Incarnation than we saw in Prayer B. A strong escha-tological memorial following the institution words leads to a clear epiclesis first over the assembly, then the gifts, yet unlike Prayer A, all in a single breath. This reflects a powerful sense that the very purpose of Communion is the sharing of the people in the priesthood of Christ and a joining together in one voice of praise. The empowerment of the people for service in Christ's name is handled differently in this Prayer; immediately following the petition to God that "we become one body and one spirit, a living sacrifice of praise," the Prayer moves to intercession for the church and the possibility of a broad set of intercessions, right in the body of the Prayer, which only then concludes with doxological praise in union with the saints.

In curating the Eucharistic Prayers, the comprehension of Prayer D really makes it appropriate for use at any time of the year, though its length and its scope commend it especially for Feasts and great celebrations. The provision of an elaborate Mozarabic tone for the chanting of this Prayer also commends its festival use. The Prayer is at its best when intercessions are included within it. One way to avoid the relocation of the intercessory prayers on a Baptismal day to a point in the service unfamiliar to Episcopalians is to use prayer D on Baptismal days, including the Intercessions within the anaphora. (See the section on Baptism, below.) Appropriate changes are also made to this Prayer in the expansive language version of Rite II (Appendix C).

Eucharistic Prayers of EOW 1

The **Eucharistic Prayers of EOW 1** are well worth considering as part of the rotation of Eucharistic Prayers that would be used over the course of a year. It is, again, something of a sport among some Episcopalians to criticize these Prayers, as we criticize anything liturgical when it is "new." (The old joke comes to mind: how many Episcopalians does it take to change a light bulb? Three: one to hold the ladder, one to change the light bulb, and one to complain about how much better the old light bulb was.) Still, they show both positive qualities and shortcomings.

All three of the EOW Prayers reflect a strong trinitarian structure, strongest in Prayers 2 and 3. **Eucharistic Prayer 1**[25] plays on themes of divine blessing and abundance, spends time on the creation of the world and of humanity, and then links our "failure to honor your image" with a brief litany of the features of that failure: "we would not see your goodness in the world around us…we violated your creation, abused one another, and rejected your love." True enough, unfortunately; but the vocabulary of this litany of our willful failures may be almost too brutal to some ears, even "triggering," so the language may be both a virtue and a shortcoming, depending on the composition of the assembly. The wise curator will take this into account. It does reflect an up-to-date sense of

---

25. EOW 1, pp. 57ff.

the social character of our sinfulness. Yet we are reassured, as in Prayer D, of God's persistence in coming to us again and again, and the Incarnation (a strong note in the Prayer, while honoring the Israelite narrative) is the culmination of a long process of deliverance, sustenance, and renewal, revealing God's glory. The cross is presented as a triumph and an "opening" of "the way of freedom and life." The genius of this section of the Prayer is its deft connection in a few words between the death of Christ and Christian discipleship. After the Words of Institution comes a straightforward epiclesis (over gifts and then assembly) that the assembly may be filled with the Holy Spirit and "live as Christ's body in the world."

The forthright language of sin makes this commendable for a penitential season or day. Yet it combines this language with a resounding proclamation of God's glory and blessing, and of triumph over evil. The combination of these two leads one priest of my acquaintance to suggest this as the perfect Eucharistic Prayer for the Easter season, with Lenten contrition still ringing in our ears, gathering theodicy within the arms of blessing. Its incarnational imagery makes it suitable for Advent, Christmas, or Epiphany, and so this Prayer turns out to be quite versatile for use.

Eucharistic Prayer 2[26] offers strong imagery around creation and maternal imagery for God, who "time and again called us to live in the fullness of your love." The second section of the Prayer, following the Sanctus and Benedictus, offers one of our sturdiest commemorations of the Incarnation, noting the significance not merely of Jesus' death but of his life—that

---

26. EOW 1, pp. 60ff.

he "broke bread with outcasts and sinners, healed the sick, and proclaimed good news to the poor." The Prayer then makes an even more important move, at once reflective of contemporary theology and classically Anglican: it makes of the sacrifice of Christ not simply his death on the cross, but *his whole manner of life*. Note the phrasing: "the time came for him to complete upon the cross the sacrifice of his life…." In Johannine fashion, the cross is the completion of the whole arc of the Incarnation, not a standalone event to which his life is, however commendable, simply the preface.[27]

After the Institution Words and the anamnesis and oblation, there is a straightforward epiclesis over gifts, and then a creative turn consistent with the Prayer's opening attention to creation, an epiclesis over the whole earth that we might be "a new creation, the Body of Christ given for the world you have made." That turn will excite some and trouble others, depending on their views of the place of creation in Christian soteriology, but it is quite biblical. The Prayer concludes with a fine vision of the diverse kingdom to come, using the language of the book of Revelation regarding "every tribe and language and people and nation" around the throne.

There is one error of voicing in Prayer 2 that one might, with a bishop's permission, consider changing: in the post-Sanctus the prayer speaks of "Jesus, the holy child of God." Given that the Prayer is an address to God, the line should arguably be prayed "Jesus, your holy child." At any

---

27. I have written more about this elsewhere. See James Farwell, "Salvation, the Life of Jesus, and the Eucharistic Prayer: An Anglican Reflection and Proposal." *Liturgy*, 31.3 (April 2016), 19-27.

rate, Prayer 2 might really be used at any time of the year, balancing as it does attention to creation, a salvific view of the life of Jesus completed in his death, the fulsome epiclesis, and a strong eschatology.

Perhaps the most creative Eucharistic Prayer in our current repertoire is EOW 1's **Eucharistic Prayer 3.**[28] Christians have long favored the trope of "the law and the prophets" in our theology and prayer and the themes of the third great portion of the Hebrew Scriptures—the Ketuvim, or Writings—has been limited in our rhetoric. This is of course the repository of the wisdom literature and this is the background to the language of Prayer 3. The most poetic of the three Prayers, the Prayer links the wisdom of God to the Word who is Jesus, through whom (following John 1) the world was created. There is rich language around creation, which is a sacramental sign of hope for human life. After the Sanctus, the Prayer links the call of the people Israel to Jesus as redeemer, deliverer from sin, and reconciler. After what is probably the most comprehensive anamnesis and oblation in all our Prayers, the epiclesis over the gifts is followed by an epiclesis of some creativity: "Grant that we, burning with the Spirit's power, may be a people of hope, justice, and love."

In addition to this beautiful Prayer's distinctive language, there is a rubrical change to this Prayer that is worthy of note: the rubric requiring that the presider touch the bread and wine at the Words of Institution is eliminated for the first time since the 1559 prayer book. This reflects not the battles over the presence of Christ that characterized that time, but the current

---

28. EOW I, pp. 62ff.

appreciation for the wholeness of the Eucharistic Prayer combined with an Anglican appreciation that it is God who consecrates and the whole Prayer that petitions for it. While the absence of the rubric does not prevent those presiders who wish to do so from touching the bread and wine, it does free the presider to consider other manual acts, including the possibility of being in the orans throughout the entire Prayer.

This Prayer, like Eucharistic Prayer 2, is capacious enough in its themes to be used at any time but might be especially apt for the Incarnation cycle and at Easter, given the Johannine emphasis of the lectionary during that season.

Now, with these Eucharistic Prayers given a thorough if not exhaustive review, we turn to the remainder of the Eucharistic rite. A decision must be made about which form of the **Lord's Prayer** will be used. As with respect to the contested language in the Creed, I remind the reader that we are dealing here with the challenges of translation. From the standpoint of the Aramaic original conveyed in a Greek text, the contemporary Lord's Prayer is arguably a closer (though not perfect) English rendering of the meaning of the original prayer, but it does not come as easily to the tongue of many who will have memorized the "traditional" form from their youth. Many the curator will make a choice here, between more faithfulness and intimacy in translation and more familiarity in language.

Sending Rite

Following Communion, there is an important choice to be made regarding music either before or after the post-Communion prayer, but I address that in the chapter on best practices in the Eucharist. The sending rite then proceeds with a **post-Communion prayer** for which four choices are possible. All are quite good and all have a parallel, bifold structure: thanksgiving for our being made one with Christ through Communion, and a petition that we be empowered as the church in the world. The first of the two in the 1979 book is probably the most widely used by Episcopalians, likely due as much to its position on the page and its brevity as to its language. The second offers a longer elaboration of thanksgiving for the gift of Communion and uses more traditional Anglican language for it; the third, in EOW 1,[29] is similar to the first, and the fourth (also in EOW) is both the most brief and the most contemporary. All four commendably deploy the clear terminology of *sending*.

A **sacerdotal blessing** is an optional element of the Rite II Eucharist. (It is required in Rite I.) Count this author among those who feel that the blessing is a questionable action by the priest; having just received the body and blood of the Lord, what possible need can the assembly have for a priestly blessing? Yet, the way the blessing has come to function is as a kind of final act of sending before the Dismissal, and the wise priest finds a way to phrase the blessing in a way that makes it clear that the *sending is the point*. That latitude exists in Rite II, as the blessing is simply present as a rubric and it is left to the priest to determine its form. Among guides for this act, the Rite I blessing is available; there are a number that are passed around as the common inheritance of the church, and one can find useful guides in Christian literature. For

---

29. EOW 1, pp. 69-70.

example, one might adapt the words of Augustine's sermons: "Become what you have received; and the blessing of God…." The presider might adapt the intro to the blessing around the words of Scripture or the Sermon just heard that day. The BOS provides a number of seasonal blessings, some of which are stronger than others in emphasizing mission, but they are useful in joining other seasonal adjustments that drive home the themes of the year. EOW 1 provides several as well, but here the EOW material is at its weakest. Most of these prayers reflect a modalism that falls outside the trinitarian doctrine we share, though they could arguably be corrected quite simply by inserting a reference to "one God."[30]

The **Dismissals** given in the prayer book provide a nice range, from simple to elaborate, depending upon the season or occasion, and are fairly straightforward to curate.

An Order for Celebrating the Holy Eucharist

The form on page 400 of the prayer book, for which supplements are also offered in EOW1, was originally intended for use on occasions when the assembly might want to take a hand in the composition of the ritual text of the Eucharist and has been commonly used as such in parish retreats or camp settings. Notwithstanding its rubric, General Convention made a decision in 2018 to allow this form to be used for the principal service on a Sunday *as long as the permission of*

---

30. E.g., "Holy eternal Majesty, Holy incarnate Word, Holy abiding Spirit, Bless you for evermore" could be taken in the direction of our received faith by inserting "triune God, ever One," or similar, between the third and fourth lines of the blessing.

the bishop is obtained. Liturgical leaders working in parishes in certain contexts, church plants, intentional communities, and other environments might find the use of this form helpful. On the other hand, with such a range of liturgical materials with which this book is dealing, and more being generated with every General Convention, and by the leave of this or that bishop, one could ask whether such an open form is helpful, and whether allowing for the construction of such singular local liturgies stretches the bonds of "common prayer" rather too far. In any case, the planner who uses this form will want to work carefully within the rubrics and may find that some of the elements left to the local community can be drawn from our already approved resources, even if others are not.

Holy Baptism

The work of planning is fairly simple in working with the Baptismal rite. It involves not so much curation as a decision about three choices with the elements already given in the rite: the use of Chrism, the order of the handlaying/chrismation and post-Baptismal prayer, and the placement of intercessory prayers and their form. The use of Chrism is an option in the prayer book, as it was a restoration from earlier practice, but the modern Episcopal Church took to it and it is now so widely used as to render further comment unnecessary. The placement of handlaying/chrismation and the post-Baptismal prayer is important but it is addressed below, in the chapter on best practices in Baptism. The intercessory prayers are too often left out of the Baptismal rite, and the rubric concerning the prayers on page 310 overlooked. After the newly baptized (and confirmed, if applicable) are welcomed, the Peace is then exchanged. Following the Peace the liturgy continues, according to this rubric, with the Prayers of the People or the Offertory. Admittedly this rubric is not crystal clear, but it seems hard to defend that on a day when new members of the community are baptized, we would shirk the assembly's prayers for all in need. There are two ways to manage this: one is to continue with the prayers immediately before the offering and preparation of the Table. Though this will feel unfamiliar to the assembly, the offering of Intercessions leading directly into the Eucharistic Prayer is a pattern not unknown to earlier prayer books. The more serviceable way to proceed is arguably to use Prayer D for a Baptismal day—certainly appropriate given what I have said above about Prayer D—and then to fold the Intercessions for the day into the appropriate place in the Eucharistic Prayer. What we ought *not* do is leave out the intercessory prayers entirely.

Conclusion

I have not touched here every feature of every rite, nor every contested issue, nor every tiny revision of the new trial rites. Subsequent chapters address some matters I have not touched here. But I have named here what I consider especially signif-icant for the well-informed curator of liturgy to think about. It is also important to be in touch with one's bishop regarding forms she or he authorizes at this time. Of course the prayer book is a given and no permissions are required there. It is wise to be in touch with the bishop about all other uses.

Having considered the forms above, it is legitimate to ask: what goes into the decision to use one form over another? What criteria are there for curation? I have alluded above to some factors that might push one way or another on certain choices, but can we identify something in the way of *general* considerations for discernment?

CHAPTER

4

Considerations in Curating Ritual Forms

W hat does the competent curator have in mind when planning liturgy? What follows is my own sense of the chief criteria we bring to bear on this task. My intention is to offer some basic considerations and then draw out of this reflection a list of basic guidelines for curating and planning.

The Givens in Liturgical Planning

We might begin with the givens, hopefully no less important for being obvious. The givens for curating and planning are the liturgical season, the liturgical day, and the appointed lections.[1] The seasons have certain themes, as do the day and the lections and these are on the whole mutually reinforcing though by no means univocal. The themes may themselves vary over the course of the season. An example is the movement from eschatological judgment early in Advent to a focus on the birth of Jesus later in the season. This movement is a function in part of

---

1. Occasionally the lectionary itself provides options, so that the lections themselves are curated.

our experience of nearing Christmas, and in part of the lections themselves which put forward these themes. In other words, there is a bit of a "chicken-egg" process in liturgical planning, since the themes inbuilt to the seasons shape the elements we curate, but the elements we curate give a significant part of the thematic density to the season. So we consider the various parts of the service in relation to the lectionary themes, which are in turn both reflective and creative of the liturgical year. Planning practices that move well within those themes is the general rule. The same goes for attending to the lections appointed for the day and the particular day in the calendar for which they are appointed.

But let us consider this point that the themes of lections, day, and season are not simply univocal. There is not simply a mutually reinforcing sameness that we see in the relationship among these on any given day, nor among the appointed lections and the elements we curate. The selection of an appropriate Acclamation, psalm setting, hymnody, form of Confession, Eucharistic Prayer, post-Communion prayer and the like may be approached in two ways: both for their complementarity and for their diversity.

With complementarity in view—sticking with our Advent example—the Advent Acclamation might be coupled with the Eucharistic Prayer one considers most to exhibit themes of longing, hope, liberation from bondage, or the coming kingdom. One might look specifically within the lections for themes that are echoed in the Eucharistic Prayer. But a different kind of liturgical action might occur if one couples a penitential Acclamation with the same Eucharistic prayer, or, a Eucharistic Prayer with a fairly conventional framing of sin and salvation—say, Prayer A—with the Advent Acclamation and music full of longing for the eschatological end. As noted in chapter two, ritualization sets into motion a whole range of images, metaphors, and (secondarily) ideas that dance and play with one another, sometimes in agreement, sometime in contestation, pushing and pulling with and against one another. This is as it should be, as we enter through liturgy into a multivalent tradition in which the play of images with and against one another deepens our capacity to navigate our lives in a complex world.[2]

Certainly, one ought not go out of one's way to plan a liturgy in which the elements one curates for that liturgy are utterly in contradiction to one another. Yet, it is hard to do so, because as long as one is working with the authorized forms, all are rooted in, and enact, the complex lifeworld that is Christianity. Perhaps the moral is this: we aim to curate forms and plan liturgies in ways that the forms, whether complementary or diverse, show a capacity to "talk" with one another. The subthemes of one might be the major themes of another; the voice of one might be a counter sign to the other. In curating and planning we aim for a coherence among the forms without looking to seek their identity or force them to yield only a single theme. (The rites themselves sometimes guarantee this holy contestation: think of Ash Wednesday, when the appointed gospel cautions us about outward action and exhorts

---

2. Scripture itself works this way. The Scriptures do not speak with one voice, but in complement and in contest, joined by the quest for the Holy One by which they are united. A fine and fuller account of this is given by Gordon W. Lathrop; see *Saving Images: The Presence of the Bible in Christian Liturgy* (Minneapolis: Fortress Press, 2017), esp. ch. 5.

us not to mark our faces as a display of piety… after which we mark our faces with ash!)

Context

The observance of the givens of liturgical year, the liturgical day, and the lectionary reading does not occur in a vacuum. These occur within a context: a culture and its norms and struggles, the daily happenings that we follow in the news and with our neighbors, the particular challenges and tasks of the members of the assembly as they move through their days. There are church wide preoccupations and there are the burdens and joys of the particular members. The effective pastor is not sealed off in a study with the Scripture, choosing hymns or forms for Confession in the abstract, or on the basis of personal preference, but listening and watching with their congregation and bearing in mind what the pastors know about those in their care. In this context, they choose hymns and liturgical forms that may reflect or challenge, console or provoke, as the context calls for. Planning liturgy in this way is a practice and skill cultivated over time, and through such planning, the dance deepens between the lections that are heard, the hymns that are sung, the prayers that are said, the exhortations that are given, and the lives we lead.

Curating and planning with an eye to context does not yield the same outcome in *every* context. One might say as a general rule that a parish Eucharist on the heels of the horrifying death of George Floyd that offers no acknowledgement of this liturgically—in the prayers, or with the use of a Eucharistic Prayer like, say, EOW prayer 1—is missing the importance of context in liturgy. On the other hand, the parish that suspends every canon of day and season and lectionary and shapes a liturgy around a single note of outrage or lament may not be setting out a healthy practice of worship either. And yet even to that general rule a rejoinder is possible: what of the liturgical worship of an African American community in Minneapolis the Sunday after Floyd's death? OR, contrariwise, a community in Vermont whose Senior Warden has died suddenly of a heart ailment in the same week? In the second case, might a different reality need to come to the foreground, with a moment to mark the death of George Floyd coming later in due time?

Rules of thumb for planning liturgy that apply across all contexts are hard to come by. Worship happens in the midst of life and everything it brings, good and bad. A liturgy that never changes much from one week to another is not paying much attention to the life that surrounds it; the liturgy that reflects the constantly changing news cycle is not paying enough attention to the unfailing covenant of God whose destiny for us lies beyond all that daily befalls us. Liturgy both reflects its context and also draws us out beyond it.

Another concern in curating the possible forms for liturgy is a respect for familiarity. There are elements of the liturgy that ought to change weekly, at least in parts—how could the Intercessions this week be identical to last week, if we are paying attention and taking into our prayer the needs of a changing world? And of course, hymns and lections change week to week (though some music is wisely retained for a stretch or a season… arguably service music). There are other elements that, while they could change weekly, are deprived of their power to draw us deeply into the worship of God if they do. A Eucharistic Prayer offers a whole comprehension of the salvation narrative, with each having a scope and themes in the foreground, as we saw in the last chapter. This prayer takes time for the community to inhabit, and in that time works its power on the imagination of the community. Changing the Eucharistic Prayer every week seems patently unwise. Arguably there are elements whose power of expression lies somewhere between familiarity and novelty. The post-Communion prayer might be an example; its content is *structured* identically across the four options as we saw in the last chapter, and changing them every three weeks or so might keep that moment of the liturgy fresh. But familiarity and recognizability, as the life-blood of ritualization, has a general precedence.

There is another vein of familiarity besides the structural feature of ritual, and that is the familiarity *of* the assembly *with* particular forms. Music planning is the most amusing (and sometimes exasperating!) dimension of liturgical practice in which it is best to work largely within the range of what the assembly knows, but not exclusively! It is also good to bring new music—the same for Acclamations, responses to the Word, Confessions, and the like—in appropriate proportion to the liturgy as well. Worship only with forms that are known, becomes moribund, and it does so because, like the body of a person, the Body of Christ flourishes with a diverse spiritual diet. The things of God are Mystery, and beyond our telling; they require our telling to take many different forms of expression. Again, constant change will not yield hearty worship that also feeds the community that offers it; but neither will a steadfast refusal ever to pray or to sing in fresh words.

Closely related, the wise curator will know the "canon

within the canon" of the community they serve. They will also know what the people love, and what they don't. Traditions that are dear can nourish, even if too much of an attachment to them risks idolatry. The rule of thumb that *some* proportionate change is healthy and necessary still applies. But it is an act of love for the planner and presider to learn the patterns and customs of the community, both in the forms they use and in the practices of the liturgy itself. Of course, there is the question of *when* to lead a community into any change. It is an old bit of wisdom (if that is what it is) passed around in the church that a priest new to a community should not change a thing in their patterns and practices of worship (or anything else) for the first full year. This deserves some consideration. However, there is a counterpoint to this bit of wisdom: in the first year of a new Rector or Priest-in-Charge, the congregation actually *expects* some change. Commonly, the community has just spent months or even a few years reflecting on places where the congregation needs growth and for which they have likely hired this very priest! In general, one should get to know the people, come to love them, and then begin to bring change; but an absolute refusal to invite the congregation into any change at all within the first year is liable to increase the resistance when the time comes that change is warranted.

Another matter to which the wise curator will attend is their relative proportion of use of the BCP and EOW. The BOS takes care of itself, as it provides forms for very specific purposes; but some congregations will need to worship primarily with the BCP, only occasionally supplemented by EOW. Others may have a higher threshold for experimenting with new forms. We will never become familiar with new forms by waiting to use them, but pacing the introduction of new material is crucial.

Another matter of increasing significance to the Episcopal Church is a respect for ethnic, racial, and national diversity. This can be complicated. On the one hand, there may be tendencies in a given racial or ethnic community toward, say, different expressions of emotion, more openness to spontaneous interjections in the liturgy (or an absolute resistance to it!), more of a preference for certain music, and so on. The wise curator of liturgical forms will bear these in mind. On the other hand, *assuming* that a particular church, because it is mostly, say, African-American or Vietnamese or Latinx in membership, has a particular liturgical style or preferences is a mistake. There is no one-for-one correspondence between specific forms of liturgical style and racial or ethnic identity, even though there may also exist some traditional racial, ethnic, or cultural distinctives. An African-American church may be Anglo-Catholic and use only the Rite I; an Anglo congregation may dance in the aisles at the Gloria and shout Amen during the Sermon. The liturgical curator will come to know her people, and develop liturgical forms accordingly.

A final thought before attempting to draw out some principles from this broad reflection: It is deeply important that clergy educate the assembly about their liturgical forms. The liturgy belongs to the assembly, not to the expert. That will only ever be the actual case, and not simply an ideal, if the community understands its resources, its heritage, the theology of its practices. The work of continuous education is central to the work of the priest (check the canons!). There is never a lack of something to teach a community, as its liturgical life is dynamic and always ongoing.

General Guidance

So, what can we say about the general principles around curating forms and planning liturgies?

- Curate forms according to the thematic emphases of seasons, days, lections. This is the basic architecture of our liturgical life.
- In paying attention to seasons and occasions, plan any given season with an eye to the whole year. It is the differential relationship of each season to all the others that gives coherence to the entire cycle.
- Seek coherence in curating among optional forms, but do not seek sameness or absolute consistency. All elements don't have to "match." We are a tradition of both agreement and contestation, identity and diversity, unity across difference, and we should expect to enact this in our liturgical forms.
- We seek a God who is at once given to us, and a holiness beyond us. Be literate in the full range of liturgical resources, and their use. This is essential to nourishing a rich spiritual imagination, and an entry into worship of One who lies beyond our words and actions.
- The familiarity of forms authorized by a community larger than us is central to ritualization. Too much change, or too frequent, ceases to have the ritual power for formation. The default is repetition, laced with some fresh expression.

Anything more and liturgy in a late modern context will become mere entertainment.

- Absolute rigidity in ritual forms is idolatry. Stretch the congregation's spiritual diet, little by little, with change.
- Teach, teach, teach… about what we do, where it comes from, why we do it.
- Know that good curation and planning is an art, not arithmetic; and we learn to do it by practice, by listening, and by much, much prayer.

CHAPTER

5

General Principles
and Best Practices

The material in the following chapters is a developed version of materials I have used and continuously revised over the years for students preparing for ordination, in classes designed to teach the arts of planning for and presiding over liturgy. I have revisited these materials in light of the decisions made by the last two General Conventions concerning liturgy. The style of this material aims at a bit of humor and is at times deliberately provocative. This is in part to jolt students out of the expectation that because they have attended liturgies for years, they will, by simply stepping out of the pew and into the presider's chair, know how to do this well. I hope that this style will accomplish a similar purpose for the readers of this book. Readers familiar with the earlier work of the Catholic liturgical theologian Aidan Kavanagh will recognize his influence on my approach,[1] though the good humor and sensibility of my own teachers, Thomas Talley and J. Neil Alexander, certainly influenced me as well. In the end, though indebted to these and other teachers, I am solely

---

1. Aidan Kavanagh, *Elements of Rite: A Handbook of Liturgical Style* (Collegeville: Liturgical Press, 1982).

responsible for what follows. It is rooted in my own experience as a presider, including many of my errors and failures, over my own years in parish leadership and in nearly 30 years of teaching. All that follow is, so far as possible, consistent with what I have said above about the features of ritual. But what follows also leans even more unapologetically into the theology of liturgy and of Christian liturgy's theology. It is, I hope, a fair revisitation of good principles for celebration for those who have been planners and presiders for just a few years, and a refresher for those who have been at this work a long time.

"Best practices" is a tricky term—tricky because the only way "best practices" emerge in any field, and the only way they are adjudicated, is by the trying and testing of a community of practitioners, and they remain open and evolving as they continue to be practiced. Perhaps when I refer to best practices, the reader can take this to be my *offering of candidates for* best practice. That said, they do emerge not only from my own experience but from that of the colleagues from whom I have learned. I have been privileged over the years to know practitioners far more gifted and skilled than I as planners and presiders. Still, both what they have taught me, and what I try and teach students, is open to contestation. I welcome this contestation. Wherever the reader feels that I have misstepped, the style of provocation in which I offer these will encourage you to push back, and articulate your own reasoning rooted in your own ministry context.

Ritual and Liturgical Principles

Ritual is the performance of the world as it truly is, or might be, or ought to be, or is coming to be. This is the cross-cultural, cross-traditional nature of ritual. Christians are not so exceptional that their ritual is, somehow, something different than everyone else's. At the same time, we have the terms of our own worldview, the very worldview enacted in our rituals, to speak of this, under the signs and symbols of our own Christian tradition. From one angle of view, we enact the world as God has brought it into new being: reconciled, redeemed, for which we give thanks. From another angle of view, we enact a world that we know is not yet here, a work begun but unfinished: we know the world in which we live is not one that acclaims God, that listens for God's Word, not one in which we make Peace with one another and share at a Table of unity. This is, as the term has it, the "eschatological" nature of liturgy. As Don Saliers puts it, in liturgy we bring "the pathos of the world into the ethos of God."[2] There we know both its final destiny of healing, but also the longing for that destiny to come. Thus, as above: "the world as it truly is, or might be, or ought to be, or is coming to be." As our own vision of the coming reign of God, enacted in liturgy, changes over time—routinely deepened, expanded, or corrected—then ritualization leads to changes in ritual. This is the paradox of liturgical practice. To some partial but important degree, the "success" of a liturgical form is measured by its capacity to

---

2. Don E. Saliers, *Worship as Theology: Foretaste of Glory Divine* (Nashville, Abingdon Press, 1994), pp. 21-38.

shape a people who come to see, through that shaping, the *limitations* of the vision they enact. Ritual is generative of ritual change, even as its basic forms always come to us through a process of revision and rarely as a complete overthrowing of what has come before.

Christian Liturgy—what Christians call their central rituals— is Jesus Christ. A liturgy is a work done FOR the people, a benefaction for the common good—like the building of an aqueduct in Ancient Rome, or a great public square. As Robert Taft notes, for Christians, the one liturgy—God's liturgy—is Jesus Christ, given for the good of the world.[3] Our "liturgies" are an entrance by the Spirit into God's mission in Christ, a participation in that mission, a transformation of the world that it constitutes, the primary though not the only mode in which it occurs. When we feed the hungry, when we stand with the marginalized, this too is liturgy. But this liturgy that is our worship is the source and summit of all the liturgy that is Jesus Christ, to whom we join ourselves in Word and Sacrament. This is the celebration of the Paschal Mystery, which is the key to the whole of our prayer book.

Liturgy is the enactment of theology and ethics. In the mode of worship, liturgy sketches and rehearses the basic metaphysical commitments of Christians. (Jesus Christ, the Word of God, the *logos tou theou*; theology, our articulation of the

---

3. Robert F. Taft, "What Does Liturgy Do? Toward a Soteriology of Liturgical Celebration: Some Theses," in *Primary Sources of Liturgical Theology*, Dwight W. Vogel, ed. (Collegeville: Liturgical Press, 2000), pp. 139-148.

meaning of the *logos tou theou*, in whom the whole world is in being.)[4] We affirm there, celebrate there, in liturgy, that God is, that the world comes from God's hand as grace, that the world is beloved, fallen, redeemed, longing for the fullness of redemption. Liturgy also, through repetitive action, rehearses the basic moral dispositions of Christian character. This occurs not only through the words used in liturgy that imagine a world, but through the rite's deep structure and sequential movement, through the spatial world in which it is enacted, and through rhythms of time it sets down. These three—rite, space, and time—are our *ordo*, the deep grammar of our action and the context in which God saves. The redeemed world arises at the intersection of these three, in the vision and the performance that is liturgy—now in a mirror, darkly, later face to face.

As liturgy enacts the *true* (theology) and the *good* (ethics) of the world God is bringing into being in Christ, so it reflects the *beauty* of that world. In classical philosophy, these are the great transcendentals: the good, the true, the beautiful. In God lives the fullness of these three; in God these find their source and their measure. We spoke above of the truths we celebrate in liturgy, of the good that we practice—when we give thanks, offer praise, attend to God's speech and silence, pray for those in need, name our failures and accept God's grace, offer Peace to one another, are sustained at God's Table and go into the world to be the people we practice in liturgy, as best we can. But there is *beauty* enacted in liturgy too, the outlines of a

---

4. John 1:1-4; Colossians 1:15-17.

world redeemed. The beauty of holiness, however, involves the broken as well as the whole—more precisely the broken as it is brought into the astonishing symmetry of the reign of God, the peculiar symmetry of the God who (as the Chinese proverb has it) "writes straight with crooked lines." This is the beauty of the disfigured Christ, the one who enters into hell and opens it out with light. "To experience beauty is to have your life enlarged," as John O'Donohue put it.[5] This beauty—the beauty of God—enlarges life to its fullest abundance.

Liturgy is fundamentally corporate. There are many ascetical, catechetical, educational, devotional practices that both form and express individual piety, funded by Eucharistic practice and returning to enrich Eucharistic practice. But the Eucharist is not a practice of individual piety. The Eucharist performs and is performed by a *social body* that works as a differentiated unity. We gather in shared space; we hear the Word of God aware that we are seated with other bodies around us, listening, or struggling to listen, as we do. We sense all faces turned in the direction of the Book. We make Peace before the Eucharist with those around us, aware of a larger body beyond those in our immediate environs making Peace as we do. We may like these who join us in this peacemaking, or we may not; we may know them or, in a larger assembly, we may not, or barely so. Yet we make Peace with them because they are the ones who, through choice and happenstance, are the people God has given us. We will eat with them—not just

---

5. John O'Donohue, *Beauty: Rediscovering the True Sources of Compassion, Serenity, and Hope* (New York: Harper Perennial, 2004), p. 20.

at the same time, but from the same Table, the same food: "We who are many are One, because we share the one Bread, One Cup." The monks of certain traditions speak of the vow of stability: committing to "work out your salvation with fear and trembling" in a single community, never moving once they have professed. A non-monastic liturgical assembly does not make such a commitment of course, but something of what the monk experiences is at work here too: it is in *this* assembly, with *these* people, around this Book, Font, Table, that I enter into the Paschal Mystery.

The liturgy is not *for* anything. Liturgy is its own end. It is not aimed at education, though it will educate in the broad sense and can be reflected upon in education outside the liturgy. It is not aimed at fulfilling, calming, or inspiring the congregation, though if it is good at what it actually does, it may from time to time also do those things. The liturgy is not for "meeting the needs" of the congregation. It is not the parish's "family meal"—that is entirely too parochial a matter. The world-making of liturgy, though enacted locally, is of a universal order, and it is a function of *being in it*, giving oneself to what it performs, not doing something "with" it or using it "for" something, any more than one "uses" one's lifeworld to "do" something with life. It is an entrance into Mystery; it is its own end, in the sense that we enact there the final end that God holds out to us: reconciliation with God and one another.

Liturgy is a performance. Liturgy is not a container for words about God. Liturgy is not a script in a book. Liturgy is not the rite itself that structures it. Liturgy is the action the assembly does with the rite. Liturgy is the rite in motion. Liturgy is a bodily performance involving movement, sight, sound, scent, touch and yes, speech. The "Logos Incarnate"—Jesus Christ— our salvation and redemption, was not an idea, a contract, or an abstraction. Our salvation was a bodily performance, a person, Jesus Christ. So it is that entering into him through praise and prayer is a performance as well, to which we bring our entire bodies and use all our senses. For liturgy, as with all ritual, the meaning is in the doing, precisely as and how one does it.[6]

Best Practices

Liturgy may be formal, or informal, but it is *never* casual. Liturgy, like all ritual, is formalized, patterned behavior oriented toward the transcendent. It is what it is and does what it does by virtue of this patterned reorientation of body, speech, thought. The body is primary. The bodily postures, demeanor, and movement of liturgical ministers are elegant, collected, warm but dignified, befitting a festal occasion. (In this sense, ALL liturgies are "festal" occasions.) Movement is deliberate, pacing is steady but not rushed. None of this means liturgy is fussy or anxious; it simply means that all is done with a sense of movement and pacing appropriate to the gravitas of what we are about: nothing less than the redemption of the world by our Lord Jesus Christ.

---

6. In this section I am not using "performance" in the sense of pretending something that is not so. I am using it in the sense that ritual theorists do: it is an action, something done, and in the doing enacts the most fundamental, the most *real* that there is.

In our tradition (Anglican), but not ours only, liturgy is not really "planned;" it is "prepared for." We do not invent liturgies. There are ample opportunities provided by the liturgy of the prayer book for local instantiation, but those are coded into a form that all Episcopal Churches share. We use the received and authorized liturgies of our ecclesial community. The tyranny of individual worship teams, committees, presiders, experts, clergy, etc., "outdoing" the congregation down the street with their fresh and exciting worship ideas is a vice, because it breaks several of the fundamental principles outlined above, and others, regarding the operation and nature of ritual. It is to be avoided in a community whose liturgy, in its broad structure (*ordo*) and authorized texts, symbols, temporal structure and spatial assumptions is intended to unite us to Christ and to the broader church. This preparation for liturgy is all the more important in a time when so many resources are available to us. Everything is curated carefully with the following in mind: the lections, the particular place we are in the arc of the lectionary, the liturgical calendar, the space with which one must work, the assembly and what is happening in their lives, the culture and what is happening around us. Even when we develop liturgy in local forms, as we can these days, we are still following a received ordo, a texture of belief and a rhythm of structure that we have inherited from the tradition and carry forward in our own day.

Preparation for the liturgy occurs *in advance*. Coaching and planning at the entry door or "on the fly" in the middle of liturgy does not make liturgical ministers appear relaxed, approachable, hip, or competent, or the gospel accessible or popular. It makes the liturgy sloppy, is not (therefore) actually liturgy, and does not thereby bespeak the seriousness of the business we are about, which is nothing other than our receptivity to the *basileia tou theou* coming to birth among us. This requires our awakened and reverent attention. Like trying to build a boat while sailing it, preparing liturgical movement, timing, and procedures as-we-go only ever turns out well by accident, once in a while; on the whole, we will end up needing life-jackets.

Do not break the rubrics or change the content of the liturgy. Rubrics and directions imply and encode theology and ethics, contribute to structure and order, or both. They are part of our authorized texts and service structure and they were not developed arbitrarily. Breaking rubrics is not savvy, hip, or forward thinking. It is simply idiosyncratic and it may be arrogant; at worst, it does violence to the liturgy and replaces the shared vision encoded in the rites with one's own vision.

So, when you break the rubrics (!) or change the content, it should be for a *monumentally* good reason. That reason should be deeply informed by the other principles and best practices of liturgy, a product of consultation with the bishop, and deeply informed by the gospel. And do not be too quick to imagine that you know what the gospel is. The gospel is the good news of a kingdom (a reign, if you prefer) which is notoriously bigger, smaller, easier, harder, or other than what you imagine it to be at any given moment. The breaking of rubrics or changing of content should *never* occur; when it does, it should *rarely* become a standing practice; and if it becomes a standing practice, it *better* have kept you awake for many long nights of disciplined theological reflection on the matter before you commit to it, because you have decided that in this case you know better than the received work and wisdom of the many learned and diligent hands that were laid to the task of the construction of the prayer book and, if applicable, other authorized rites, a task that was ratified by the whole church in council. The Dalai Lama offers good general advice on breaking rules: "Learn the rules so well that you know how to break them." That little aphorism is *not* primarily meant to encourage the breaking of rules. Jesus' comments on the ox in the ditch on the Sabbath function similarly.

Anxiety (the opposite of faith) is the enemy of good liturgy. Aidan Kavanagh taught us this. If liturgy is the world as God is bringing it into new being in Christ, by the power of the living Spirit, then in liturgy we join ourselves to God in faith that nothing is lost, and all good things are already given. The first word, and the final word, is Love. To quote from an Ash Wednesday Sermon I once heard, on the eve of our grand commitment to the various disciplines for the coming season: "What if we approached all this from the position that we are loved?" We are, indeed, beloved. This means: we do not trade careful preparation in faith for neurotic obsession. Nor do we become haphazard. Chant this several times a day: *in liturgy, we seek not perfection, but excellence.*

Know the *ordo* so well you breathe it and feel it in your bones. You know it through studying, but much more through doing. Keep to the *ordo*, which I take to be the constellation of space, time and rite, and, in the rite, the movement from the Gathering of the assembly, the hearing and response to the Word of God, the celebration of the Sacrament, and the Sending. The people you lead should feel these four movements as the movement of the gospel life itself—is it not? We come together by the grace of God, hear again the Word that brings us there and begin to adjust our lives in prayer and confession; beggars all, we come to the table of God to be fed for our ongoing Baptismal conversion, and we return again to the world "in witness to [this] love."[7] Make all rubrically authorized decisions, and all decisions left to discretion by rubrical silences, in a way that allows the assembly to feel this movement. In your own gestures and movement, in the pacing you bring to each element of the rite, have in mind—*in body*—that this ordo is felt as it moves. Linger long enough on each element in accordance with its degree of centrality and then move the sequence along. (For example, a 10 minute processional hymn and a 3 minute homily would not be in keeping with the relative significance of the parts of the *ordo*.) Liturgical leadership serves the *ordo*. When you cease to do that, you cease to be Anglican, and you risk ceasing to be Christian. Yes, the *ordo* has that much to do with the gospel itself!

To expand: keep the ordo of time, by way of the calendar of the Episcopal Church in your local context. In terms of the weekly cycle, we have Principal Feasts, Sundays (Feasts of Our Lord), and Major Feasts, only three of which Major Feasts trump the Sunday propers *when they fall on the Sunday:*

---

7. BCP, the prayers for the candidates at Baptism, p. 306.

The Holy Name, The Presentation, and the Transfiguration.[8] These rules of precedence fix the temporal rhythm of liturgical life. All other Feasts and observances are optional, but the optional should be set into some sort of fixed rhythm that is logical for the community that observes them and does not work against the *ordo* of time. In terms of the annual cycle, we have an Incarnational and Paschal Cycle, in relation to which Principal Feasts make sense. *Keep the cycles.* We live our lives in time and space, and creating an idiosyncratic calendar isolates the assembly from the wider Episcopal Church and, in some cases, even from the church catholic.

Keep to the ordo of space. There are three centers around which the assembly moves—figuratively for sure, but preferably literally moves as the overall space allows: The Font, the Ambo, the Altar/Table. In these three centers is encoded the basic elements of discipleship—initiation into a pattern of life, listening for the living Word of God, being continuously sustained by Christ for this life. All other appointments in the space should at least support, and better yet point to, the cardinal value of these sites. This is the sacred geography of liturgy, as what each one signifies is the landscape of our ongoing transformation. In contemporary worship spaces it is sometimes possible for the assembly to move as a whole body from one space to the next. For example, on a regular Sunday Eucharist, begin with the entrance rite at the Font, process into the pews and presider's and leader's chairs, move to the Altar at the time of the Great Thanksgiving. This will not be

---

8. BCP, p. 16.

possible for many churches, but consider whether there are small ways that you can nod to this kind of movement. For the love of all things holy, don't be moving things around all the time. Especially *do not move the liturgical centers* around (Font, Ambo, Table). Flexible space can flex all it wants—*around* the centers, which remain stable. (There is a reason why, in nine out of ten churches built to be flexible, within a year they find a place for the liturgical centers, and even for the congregational seating, which then rarely ever move. This is not a failure; this is a case of good ritual logic surfacing in the instinct of the assembly.) The stability of these centers signifies something important about the persistence and the immovable love of the God who calls us into discipleship.

Make decisions about your local customary with the last two points—about time and space—in mind. To keep the rhythm of time, set a pattern of practices that distinguish Principal Feasts from Sunday, Major, Lesser, and daily Liturgies. To keep this rhythm, modulate the following: incense, music, movement, vesture, rite. By the latter, I mean options within the rite: for example, Song of Praise, Eucharistic Prayers, use of the Penitential Rite. You "dial up" or "dial down" the solemnity of a liturgical occasion by establishing a pattern of usage of the elements above that you stick with. Think of them, if you like, as "toggles." (Don't constantly "mix and match." Changes can occur over the life of a community, but not every year, or—*God deliver us*—every month, week, or day.)

Among the procedures that are done every single time you worship, find out what works well in the space and *do it every*

time. Rooms have a logic of their own, including the "rooms" in which we do liturgy. We do not need 17 different ways of plotting out the gospel procession (maybe two or three) or getting the processional party in and out the door (maybe two or three) or preparing the Altar for Communion (probably just one way).

Liturgy should reflect the rich variety of ideas and images to which the Tradition points (Bible, historical theology and spirituality) and should (and will) unfold and incorporate new ideas and images funded by the thinking *against* the tradition *with* the tradition. Consider, the movement toward women's ordination or gender-balanced language as examples of our thinking against the tradition with the tradition's very values. Or think of the rich variety of soteriological images in the tradition. Regarding the latter, tradition speaks with many voices, and "revelation" is not alone exempt from the hermeneutic context in which we are always operating, leaving everything else to "theology." We do not worship the Bible, but the dynamic God, the Living Word, and the Ever-Moving Spirit of whom we testify. The liturgy is a living performance of a growing Church before a God who "will be who [God] will be."

CHAPTER

6

Best Practices
for the Eucharist

The Eucharist has been in one form or another central to the communal practice of Christians in both east and west, so far as the evidence will reveal, since the origins of the Jesus movement. It is, for Episcopalians, "the principal act of Christian worship on the Lord's Day and other major Feasts."[1] It is, in its entirety, a celebration in both Word and Sacrament, in which we commune with Christ in the hearing of his word and the eating of the meal in which he gives himself again and again to us. Although not widely known by Episcopalians, the Eucharist has long been understood in Christian liturgical teaching as a part of the act of initiation—a repeatable part, in which we are sustained over the course of our lives in the practice of our Baptismal commitments. Recent challenges to Eucharistic practice during the worldwide SARS-CoV2 pandemic have made clear that we have failed in our catechesis about the Eucharist in recent years and need to reengage that effort. The Eucharist is not simply an extension of the meal ministry of Jesus, nor is it primarily a fellowship meal at which the newcomer is welcomed. These

---

1. BCP, p. 13.

sorts of meals have their place. The theology of the 1979 prayer book, however, channels the theology of the Eucharist as a *post-resurrection* meal, warranted by the Last Supper accounts though not simply a repetition of it. It was understood as early as Paul's writing as a ritual enactment of the unity of those joined to the Body of Christ. Theologically—and emerging from the rite itself—the Eucharist is classically understood as a Christian commitment in the form of remembrance of Christ, thanksgiving for salvation, a sacrifice in the sense of both the offering of thanksgiving and a joining of ourselves to the benefits of Christ's one sacrifice, sacrament of the church's unity in him, medicine of the soul, communion in and with him, sanctification by the Spirit, empowerment for ministry, and ritualized hope in Christ's coming.

A note regarding the following: in all cases, as I said earlier, references are to Rite II in the prayer book, since this is the rite that the majority of communities in the Episcopal Church use for what they consider their main liturgy on Sundays.

Fundamental Practices

The Holy Eucharist occurs around Ambo, Font, and Table. Movement, seating, spatial arrangements should as much as possible be arrayed around these three centers in a way that accentuates their centrality in worship and in Christian life. The "split" Ambo (lectern and pulpit) is, even if regrettable, a manageable historical departure from this arrangement. A Font stuck in the corner—dragged out for Baptism and put away afterward—is not!

The Eucharist is a celebration in Word and Sacrament. Its ordo, most fundamentally, is fourfold: *Gathering, Word, Meal, and Sending.* Within this ordo there are further overlapping structures in the whole liturgy. The wise presider will know both this primary ordo and its overlapping constituents and will pace the liturgy in such a way that the assembly knows those levels of the ordo in their bones. Gathering, Word, Sacrament, Sending. Then, within each of these four is a rhythm of proclamation and response. The Gathering has within it an acclamation and praise of God, concluding with prayer. The liturgy of the Word has within it the readings, followed by responses in Sermon, Creed, Intercessions and Confession. The great prayer at the Table always begins in thanksgiving and remembrance of God's great acts and concludes with invocational prayer for blessing by the Spirit (epiclesis). What remains to the Sending is a final act of thanksgiving and a Dismissal. In these rhythms of proclamation and response is the broad moral shape of the Christian life: gratitude and witness. In all this, Word and Sacrament remain primary; music and liturgical selections serve to point to their primacy. Entrance and sending rites, as some of the "soft points"[2] of the liturgy, are tempting places to multiply actions and elaborate with music, movement, and other elements. Resist this temptation, especially prevalent among Episcopalians, who have been known to fetishize pageantry once in a while! These elements of the ordo serve to gather and to send—they should be felt in this way, but not as parades. Processions may be dressed up on occasion

---

2. Robert Taft, "The Evolution of the Byzantine 'Divine Liturgy,'" *Orientalia Christiana Periodica* XLIII (Rome, 1997), pp. 8-30.

as one of the liturgical "toggles" that mark the significance of a holy day.

The Altar is not cluttered with various ritual paraphernalia. The prayer book rubric indicates that the Altar is "spread with a clean white cloth." Nothing signifies so powerfully than a symbol with clean lines. Even better if one could be seated and centered initially around the Ambo and move to the Altar at the appropriate time, though few of our churches are constructed in that way. In any case, vessels, books, etc. are placed on the Altar when needed for the action at the Altar, not before... and removed after. Whether you view it as a holy Altar or a holy Table (it is multivalent, and thus both), it is definitely not a worktable, display table, or bookstand.

Liturgy is, in its most fundamental nature, sung. Spoken liturgies are, normatively speaking, acceptable but exceptional. Music is a part of the liturgy and serves it. Musical selections should be appropriate to the occasion, neither truncating nor excessively lengthening the dynamic movement of the ordo. There are many "helps" available to planners who feel they know less about music than they would like. Better yet: learn the hymnals and supplements! One does not have to be an expert in all things, but the more the planner knows, the better able they will be to work with their church musician. (These days, some musical literacy is more important than ever, as not all churches will be able to employ church musicians full-time, and not all church musicians will have the same level of training in liturgy.)

Eucharistic ceremonial, its greater or lesser elaboration (what some people still call "high" or "low," though not the original usage of the terms), should reflect the ordo of time. The ceremonial and ritual "toggles" available for distinguishing between Principal Feasts, Sundays, Major Feasts, Lesser Feasts, Ordinary days, and seasons, are: music, vesture, movement, the use of incense (except for those churches in which incense is always used), and sometimes liturgical adaptations of the rite appointed or commended for the day (e.g., renewal of Baptismal vows, litanies). Set a pattern of observance corresponding to the rhythm of the church calendar and keep to it over the cycle of the year.

The 1979 prayer book includes pages 406 to 410. Amazing what guidance these pages offer! There are both suggestions and also *prescriptions* in these pages that address preparation of the space, customs around psalmody, the proper use and timing of the Gloria (or Song of Praise that stands in for it) and/or Kyrie, notes on the work of the deacon, and various adjustments that need to be made on certain occasions. Especially invaluable are the directions for the manner in which the liturgy of Table and the Communion are conducted. These are theologically significant, not simply customary by habit, and the presider must tend to them. I will defer attention to these directions until we reach the relevant points in the liturgy of the Table, below.

Entrance Rite

Economy of movement and ceremony is a basic ritual norm.
Many Episcopal churches begin the Eucharist with a processional hymn followed by the Acclamation after the ministers
of the liturgy have reached their seats. Consider an alternative,
working with the grain of the entrance rite: invite the people to
stand; say the Acclamation from the place of entrance; offer the
Collect for Purity, if said (remember it is optional in Rite II;
see below); then process on the Gloria/Song of Praise/Kyrie,
arriving at the presider's chair in time for the Collect of the
Day, after which people sit for the readings. The upside of
this arrangement is that the entrance is cleaner, and less likely
to compete with the more important matters to follow; the
downside: you lose a hymn. Some therefore might want to try
this form of entrance, in the season of Lent or at another penitential occasion. The rare community that has a daily Eucharist
with music—for example, a monastic or educational institution—may want to consider this form of entrance as routine.
The use of the penitential order to set off certain seasons is a
good idea.

Cense the ambo, not the altar, during the entrance rite.
Though it will strike fear into the hearts of some, the customary manner of censing the altar at the entrance of the liturgical
party and/or the Gloria/Kyrie might profitably be rethought. If
the Word is the center of the first part of the liturgy, then *cense
the Ambo* at the entrance rite, just as one censes the Font at the
time of its use in Baptism, and the Altar at the time of its use for
the Sacrament. Episcopal Churches are sometimes hard pressed

to view Word and Sacrament as equally significant, rather than the Word being simply a preparation for the Table. If we take the Scripture seriously, let's cense the Ambo and Bible before the readings. This leads to the following recommendation....

The procession of a Gospel Book at the Entrance rite (and processing and reading from that book later) is not simply a given; it is a hermeneutical decision with a history and might be done otherwise. Processing the gospels separately from the rest of the Bible communicates that the gospels are the lens through which Scripture is read by Christians. Whether this practice inevitably communicates a supersessionist position in relation to Judaism is worthy of debate, but in any case, it is arguably better to carry the whole Bible in procession. While admittedly running the risk of crushing a small acolyte (which suggests that in the absence of a deacon, some other adult be its bearer), this practice communicates a different position—that the meaning of the gospel (and Jesus) is located in its longer historical, religious, and textual context, and that the gospels illuminate what God has been up to for all of history, brought to its manifestation in Christ. The is symbolically superior to the carrying of a Gospel Book as well; ideally, a single Ambo, with a single book, is the focus of all attention for this segment of the liturgy. And—see the comment below, regarding incense—the single Book, placed on the Ambo at the entrance rite, is then censed, just as we cense the altar at the appropriate time.

Processional order is adiaphora, and Jesus was reasonably clear about our preoccupation with who sits at the left and right hand of God. But that does not mean no logic applies

at all, as the procession serves a practical purpose, and some of
those processing are called to be the living sacramental symbols
of the presence of God and church to one another. In some
cases, it may be appropriate to enter quietly in the order of
seating and simply sit down for a period of silence before the
opening Acclamation. If there is a procession, no need to rein-
vent the wheel: thurifer, crucifer, torches, lay ministers (choirs,
chalicists, etc.), assisting priests, preacher, deacon(s), presider
("celebrant," i.e., bishop or presiding priest). Notice that the
deacon accompanies the presider, who stands in for the bishop.
A deacon and a presider together is the best rule. Let us hope
Jesus also likes a procession.

**God might show up in an Anglican liturgy even if the Collect
for Purity is not used.** This collect is required in Rite I but
it optional in Rite II. The Collect for Purity is lovely. As a
preparatory prayer for worship, it is somewhat illogical in its
place *within* the rite. When it is used, it creates the impression of a liturgy that starts, backs up, and starts again. While
Catherine Pickstock[3] may consider the starting and stopping
and restarting of the medieval Roman rite a kind of genius
manifestation of the limits of doxological language before the
glory of God, one might suggest instead that there is a certain
disorder here, a disruption of the flow, and we would prefer not
to imitate the bumpiness of the medieval Roman rite. Consider
using this Collect as a preparatory prayer in the vesting room;
or, if announcements are offered before the start of the liturgy,

3. Catherine Pickstock, *After Writing: On the Liturgical Consummation of Philosophy*
(Oxford: Blackwell, 1997).

conclude them with the Collect for Purity before the whole congregation, with a period of silence, before beginning the liturgy.

The Collect for Purity and the Collect of the Day are said by the presiding priest, NOT by the congregation. The recent fad of having the whole congregation say one or both of these is both a pragmatic and a theological mess. Pragmatically, the Collect of the Day is often grammatically complex, and must be said with some rhetorical and prayerful artfulness. This is what we train presiders to do. If said by the whole assembly, its members will not even hear the Collect as they muddle along trying to figure out where to pause and how to parse, stumbling over their neighbors as they try to say it together. Theologically, it reflects a confusion of the orders of ministry, a false democratization of the assembly that obscures the differentiated unity of the church to which St. Paul points—a differentiated unity reflective of trinitarian dynamics.

When bidding the Collect of the Day, the presider says, "Let us pray." Why not leave some silence before the prayer itself? While the primary purpose of the bidding "Let us pray" at the end of a dialogue between presider and people is to signal that the prayer to follow is being offered on behalf of the entire assembly, one might utilize silence there for the assembly to gather its intention. Not a long silence, but enough at the end of a fairly busy entrance rite to slow us down and get us ready for what is to follow.

The Liturgy of the Word

The readings from Scripture and the chanting (or saying) of the psalms, should be treated with the utmost preparation and delivered with clarity and reverence. This is so obvious that it seems hardly to need saying. Certainly, there are many fine readers of Scripture and leaders of psalmody. And yet, one must candidly acknowledge that the quality of reading one hears in *entirely too many Episcopal churches* is not worthy of the gravity of what is being read. Clergy and lay leadership *must* assure that those who read are those who prepare—and *only* those who prepare—and teach them the arts of reading Scripture, if needed. It should be delivered at a pace and volume that the assembly can follow; and read in a way that makes clear the reader understands the rhetorical flow and content of the text. The whole of the liturgy is evangelical in the deepest sense, and this is nowhere more true than in the proclamation of Scripture.

The Sermon is a hinge point in the liturgy: it is both response to the readings and itself proclamation of the gospel. I find myself encouraged by the quality of the preaching in Episcopal Churches these days. Those of us in the position to preach might continue to improve, especially developing skills in a range of different rhetorical forms. Scripture itself is variegated in its rhetorical genres, and the capacity to deliver a variety of homiletic genres could only be to the good. It is said that all preachers really have only one Sermon. That may be true in the sense that we each have a fundamental vision of the gospel that is presented in different ways at different times. But it is certainly true in this sense: there is one gospel, and that is Jesus Christ, crucified and risen. Everything else is elaboration of that one gospel.

The Nicene Creed is prescribed for use on Sunday mornings. The use of the Creed is hotly debated in some quarters of the Episcopal Church, and the fact that it is hotly debated anywhere would be a complete surprise to others. Among the concerns that get raised by those for whom the Nicene Creed is a problem: the theological density of its language, the fact that its current form in our prayer book reflects a western revision of the original Creed that is offensive to our eastern Orthodox siblings, and uncertainty about what, exactly, is its function in the liturgy. These are legitimate concerns to greater or lesser degree, and I address some of them in my commentary on vol. 1 of *Enriching Our Worship* in chapter three. Perhaps this is sufficient to say here: the Nicene Creed fulfills an important ritual function, getting the assembly on its feet again after hearing the Scriptures read and the Sermon preached. The sensory experience of the corporate body rising to its feet to offer its expression of a response to the Word is an excellent outcome of the use of the Creed, and unless one's bishop authorizes the use of An Order for Celebrating the Holy Eucharist in which some other such response could be deployed, we might give the benefit of the doubt to the role of a Creed that has had a powerful history of usage among Christians for a long time and reflects certain settled and important points of doctrine regarding the relationship among the persons of the Trinity.

The Intercessions are the work of a priestly people, joining themselves to Christ in his continuous intercession for the world. First order of business: It is past time to retire the forms provided for the Prayers of the People in the 1979 prayer book. Intercessions should be delivered in such a way that they do not offer prayers while the congregation listens, but invite the congregation—even *provoke* the congregation—*to pray.* Intercessors should be trained as well as lectors are, and fine examples of Intercessions can be found in *Planning for Rites and Rituals* and the ELCA's resource, *Sundays and Seasons.* (See Chapter Three.)

Confession is good for the soul. Faith in God is good for the soul. Faith in Confession is misplaced. Human beings have an extraordinary capacity to make something good into an object of attachment and thereby undermine its goodness. Confession is very much like this. It is, and should be, expected by the prayer book to be a normal inclusion in the Eucharist. (Part of the genius of our liturgy is that right in the middle of the ritual in which we practice, in the mode of praise, being who God calls us to be, we confess our repeated failures at doing just that.) That we were created with the capacity to repent is a gift from God, and so is God's forgiveness. But here's the thing: we easily slip into imagining Confession as a transaction, *since imagining life is a transaction (and not a gift) is one of our fundamental sins to begin with.* What the monks call "scrupulosity" is also a sin—being so preoccupied with our sins that we imagine we cannot approach the Altar unless we confess them first. This is to make our performance of confession into the object of our faith, rather than God's absolute freedom and intent to forgive.

Imagining that God cannot prepare us for the Altar *unless* we confess is, of course, actually *unfaith*. From time to time, as the prayer book allows, it is good for us to approach the Table without Confession included in the rite. A good candidate for this practice is to eliminate the Confession from the liturgy for the Great Fifty Days of Easter—one long celebration of the Easter truth: that we are forgiven and free, not of our own doing, but of God's gracious love.

Supplemental ritual actions can occur after the Creed, or here, or at the time between the Peace and the Offertory. In the case of the presentation of Catechumens or Candidates for Baptism, just after the Creedal affirmation seems the logical place. Other actions—the commissioning of teachers, welcoming of newcomers, and so forth—are nicely done here, so that the Peace is shared immediately with the participants in the ritual. See above, Chapter Three.

The Peace is a ritual action, not a social hour. For the love of all things holy, help members of the assembly understand that the Peace is not a social interlude, the halftime break, or intermission! The Peace is a ritual act. When we pass the Peace, we're not greeting one another as a courtesy; we are extending to others the sign of the Peace under which God, in grace, has set us. It is the Peace of Christ we share—far more profound than a polite or even hearty human exchange. The Peace should be both warm and formal, and it should not bring the assembly's movement through the rhythm of the ordo to a complete standstill. (It is not our exchange of friendliness that moves us to the Table—it is the Word of God that does so.) Note that the prayer book allows for the Peace to be shared in the Roman position, at the time of the Fraction. Episcopalians rarely do this, but one wonders if placing the Peace in the Roman position now and again—perhaps for a liturgical season—might help solidify the understanding that the Peace is not a time for extraneous chat. If *necessary* announcements must occur here (or anywhere) keep them brief. Only necessary announcements, preferably delivered in a style that does not feel like an intermission.

The Liturgy of the Table

The central act of the Offertory is the preparation of the Table and Offering… not a seven layered procession, a choral concert, or the weekly opportunity to sing "Old One-Hundredth." This is another one of those moments in the liturgy that Robert Taft called "soft points"—places where all manner of insertions get made over time, which eventually distorts and misshapes the ordo. The assembly should have every chance here to feel the anticipation of moving to the holy Table. That's it. A well-chosen choral offering or hymn—not too long—a collection of offerings— central to the Eucharist from early on, through offerings for the poor—and the laying out of the vessels, is all we need to do here. If at all possible, bread and wine should always come up from the assembly as part of the offering. Real bread is commendable, but getting the right recipe that will hold together while being broken and replicating that recipe weekly is crucial.

The Altar/Table is prepared with a single paten and chalice, and any vessels necessary to be sufficient for the assembly. I am happy to report that most deacons and presiders prepare the Altar well. I am disturbed to report that enough do not that it requires this reminder. Here is where we pay some attention to the directions on pages 406-410 of the prayer book, as earlier promised. We will be following those directions closely below as well, with respect to procedures for communicating the assembly. There is a practical symbolics in the 1979 prayer book to the manner in which we set the table and prepare the elements for Communion. Let's call it a "One-Many-One" logic. The altar is, so far as possible if there is a flagon with the necessary amount of wine, marked by the visual of a *single paten* and (especially, given sight lines) a *single chalice*. The time to prepare any additional vessels to facilitate Communion *comes later*—after the Fraction and before the Invitation. (Look at the rubrics!) The deacon sets the Table. While the prayer book allows for other priests to assist, in the absence of the deacon it is perhaps a better model to have the presider set the Table.

In the event that incense is used, the Altar is censed. As with all liturgical movement, economy is the order of the day. Cense the vessels; walk around the Altar and cense. If desired, one can end with an additional trinitarian censing of the vessels, though this is not necessary. The priest is a member of the assembly and can be censed together with the rest of the Altar party if space allows it. (In fact, censing the priest separately may suggest a certain clericalism.) Be sure to cense the people in the pews: if we are preparing "holy things for holy people," then the people should always be censed as well. If you can't or won't cense the whole assembly, for whatever reason, *do not cense anything or anyone.*

This is a Feast. If at all possible, sing. We sing on festal occasions. The Feast of Our Lord Jesus Christ is always a festal occasion.

The Eucharistic Prayer is… a prayer. It is not meant to be read; it is meant to be *prayed*. At the Sursum Corda, the presider appropriately makes eye contact with the people; after establishing this contact, it is not appropriate to look up at the people. Whatever we learned in public speaking, it is plain weird for the presider to be looking at the people while offering the Prayer to God; in fact, depending on the point in the Eucharistic Prayer when the presider's eyes happen to fall on the people, it can be downright disturbing. (Presiders should always be attentive to the point where they are in the liturgy and voice accordingly. When bidding, exhorting, or inviting: make eye contact; praying: look upward or at the book. Just make sure you are *praying* what is there.) The Eucharistic Prayer is the longest set piece of the liturgy, and a good presider has taken its theology on board, knows its rhetorical rise and fall, and prays it in a bold voice, neither yelling nor mumbling. The latter suggests you are doing something that does not concern the congregation; the former does not inspire the congregation's faith—it simply gives the impression you are trying to talk yourself or the assembly into enthusiasm about God.

Manual acts during the Eucharistic Prayer should be carefully considered. The presider is not doing a magic show;

much crossing and waving and lifting and bowing gives the impression that you are up to some sort of esoteric ceremony. Economy of movement is better, and only where illustrative of what is being prayed, helping to bring home the rhythm of the prayer to the assembly and focusing on principal actions. It is the whole prayer that does the work to invite the presence of God and express the assembly's faith and desire for that presence, not special signs at special moments made by the priest, nor play-acting as if one is Jesus at the Last Supper. The Anglican prayer book tradition has since 1662 instructed the priest to touch the bread and wine at the Words of Institution, following the Roman theology of the sacramental conversion "occurring" as a result of the utterance of the Words—even though this is difficult to support from the standpoint of contemporary scholarship regarding the composition and shape of the Eucharistic Prayer.[4] One Prayer, the third in EOW 1, eliminates that rubrical requirement to touch the bread and wine at the words, which open up the possibility that presiders might make a different choice, and perhaps we might consider that in the future other Eucharistic Prayers would allow for other choices—for example, simply the extension of the hands over the gifts and people at the epiclesis, or remaining in the orans the entire Prayer, perhaps with a simple bow at the

---

4. As background, see David R. Holeton, ed., *Renewing the Anglican Eucharist: Findings of the Fifth International Liturgical Consultation* (Cambridge: Grove Books, 1995). The Words of Institution are better understood as the final moment of the Prayer's thanksgiving and remembrance (rather than a consecratory formula), before moving to the petitionary section of the Prayer, including the epiclesis (invocation of the Spirit). Any straight reading of the rhetorical structure of the Eucharistic Prayer would concede that, seeking the apex of the prayer, it is the epiclesis through to the Great Amen that one finds.

Great Amen.[5] My own choice, these days, is orans until the Words of Institution, non-dramatic touch of the vessels while they remain on the altar (what do you imagine you are doing when you elevate it above your head?), generous gesture with open hands over the gifts and the people at the epiclesis (in the order called for by the Prayer), and one solemn bow at the Great Amen. There are other acceptable ways, depending on theology and piety and space and so on. Wherever one lands on a decision about manual acts, presiders might profitably ask themselves: why am I doing these actions, and for whom and what purpose? Who actually does the action in the Eucharist?

The Great Amen, otherwise known as the People's Amen, is… the *people's* Amen. The more the presider says the People's Amen, the less robustly they will say it. Allow the people to ratify the Eucharistic Prayer you have just prayed on behalf of us all.

Leading the Lord's Prayer is a bit like singing in the choir: make sure you are heard, but make sure you can hear the parts around you. Use the correct bidding for the Lord's Prayer, whether traditional or contemporary, and then *lead* the Lord's Prayer. It is common mistake among presiders to bid the Lord's Prayer and then drop one's own volume so far that the congregation cannot hear you, and then the congregation falters in their own praying. Obviously, do not speak the Lord's

---

5. For relevant reflections, see Louis Weil, *Liturgical Sense: The Logic of Rite* (New York: Seabury, 2013), esp. chs. 7 and 8. I commend Weil's entire book to the reader, as I do Juan Oliver's *The House of Meanings: Christian Worship in Plain Language* (New York: Church Publishing, 2019).

Prayer so loudly that only you can be heard, but do not forget that you are still leading… so, lead.

The Fraction does not break the body of Jesus—he is crucified but already resurrected and ascended. The Fraction is the initial act in preparing the bread for distribution, linking the sacrifice of Christ to the Communion of the people. The Breaking of the Bread is *done in silence.* Too often the said or sung anthem happens immediately upon breaking. Do not fear silence: let the breaking be seen and (depending on the bread) perhaps heard, and then let the anthem be said or sung. (See the rubric on page 364 of the prayer book: it is directive, not permissive, that a "period of silence is kept" at the Fraction). In fact, it is the *anthem* that is optional, even if common in Episcopal Churches. It is unnecessary to break the bread and wave it in the air. Are we showing it to God (who is apparently on the roof)? To what end? Raise the bread *in front of you* so the people can see the action, to a height appropriate to the space, and break it simply but clearly; as the choir/congregation begins the Fraction Anthem, proceed with the breaking up of the bread while the deacon and or assisting ministers bring the additional vessels to the Altar. This should happen *prior to the Invitation to Communion*—not simply because it is peculiar to issue the invitation to eat before the food is ready, but because this is the second moment when the One-Many-One dynamic unfolds: the one bread, which will be for us the Body of Christ, now broken so that many can partake, by which in the eating the Many are made one. This is a theology of Eucharist as old as the New Testament and the Didache. See, again, the important directions on page 407 of the prayer book: "During the Great Thanksgiving, it is appropriate that there be only one chalice on the Altar, and, if need be, a flagon…from which additional chalices may be filled after the Breaking of the Bread."

Contrary to common practice: after the Invitation to Communion, the people immediately begin moving toward the Altar as the presider receives and communicates the other ministers of the Sacrament. Communion belongs to the whole assembly. Once the Invitation is issued, it is unfortunately common in the Episcopal Church for the first rows of communicants to be "held" from going forward while the communion of the presider and altar party occur. Bad idea. The point of this ritual is the communion of the assembly, not the special communion of the priest followed by the assembly. *The presider receives first.* There is a theology to most practices (not all), and there is theology to the presider receiving Communion last, which happens in some other churches—hospitality, servant of the people, etc.—although it also reinforces the idea that there is something important about the presider's receiving that is different than everyone else's. The theology that informs this practice, though, is not ours. Two directive rubrics in our prayer book make clear that the presider, consistent with our theology of ordination, is a sacrament to the congregation of the discipleship of all; as someone once put it, "a priest is just like everyone else, only more so." The priest receives as an act of discipleship and does not deign to administer Communion and its grace to others before receiving herself (and the same goes for the other ministers of the Sacrament.) *At the same time,* *the congregation can be moving to join the action, so we do not make more of this than we should.* The rubrics are worth quoting in full here. From page 365 of the prayer book: "The *ministers receive the Sacrament* in both kinds and then *immediately* deliver it to the people." To understand how the people could receive "immediately," this, from our now familiar additional directions on page 407: "*While the people are coming forward* to receive Communion, the *celebrant [presider] receives* the Sacrament...." (Emphases added.)

The assembly receives from the Eucharist celebrated by that assembly. Additional bread and wine is often kept in an aumbry, primarily in our tradition for the Communion of the sick between Sunday services. We do not load the aumbry with bread and wine to use the "following" Sunday after their consecration. The Eucharist is not a hoarding exercise. Consecrate the appropriate amount of bread and wine for the assembly gathered before you. Of course, if you undercount by accident—which happens to all of us—the aumbry provides a backup, but one may also consecrate additional elements using the formula on page 408 of the prayer book. The latter should be done quickly and without fanfare—use the short form provided there. There is no need to draw attention to priestcraft in the middle of Communion.

Speaking of those who are ill or otherwise unable to attend: Lay Eucharistic Visitors are the next best thing. There is much to be said for the practice of taking Communion to those absent for good reason immediately following the Sunday liturgy. This lifts up the significance of the assembly. These days, those unable to attend might well watch and hear the liturgy livestreamed and then receive from Lay Eucharistic Visitors, heightening their sense of being connected to the assembly, even though they cannot be a part of it. (Eucharistic assembly, in the Christian sacramental tradition, is real-time and embodied.)[6] We have a form for this practice which can be found on p. 62 of second volume of *Enriching Our Worship*: "In the name of this congregation, I send you forth bearing these holy gifts, that those to whom you go may share with us in the Communion of Christ's body and blood. We who are many are one body, because we all share one bread, one cup." As this practice of Lay Eucharistic Visitation is an extension of the act of Communion, the appropriate time for conveying the bread and wine to those who will take it is *immediately after* the Communion of the people and *before* the post-Communion prayer. (And the Lay Eucharistic Visitors should take the sacrament immediately or as soon after the service as the condition of the intended communicant allows.)

The people did not need to watch the ministers of Communion receive before moving toward the altar; they do not need to watch the ministers consume any remaining sacramental elements after. After Communion, immediately and reverently place vessels with bread and wine back on the credence table or convey them to the sacristy. Remaining elements can be consumed reverently after the liturgy. At this point in worship,

---

6. See all the essays in "Revisiting Sacramental Theology in the Wake of a Pandemic," ed. by James Farwell, a special focus issue of *Anglican Theological Review* (Winter 2022).

the people have received, and the most important thing to do is get out the door.

The Sending Rite

Did I mention that the most important thing to do is get out the door? Here things get a little tricky in Episcopal Churches. If one follows the prayer book rite itself, the congregation has heard music, anthems, and/ or sung hymns or psalms during Communion, and what is left is simply to give thanks for being made members of Christ and sustained by the Sacrament; ask for strength to participate in the mission of God in the world; and be dismissed to go. The proximity of Communion to Dismissal is deliberate; we have received the Body of Christ, and so we are dismissed to *be* the Body of Christ in the world. But what happens in most churches is that there is a processional hymn added into this sending sequence—another one of Robert Taft's "soft points" of the liturgy. There is a permission in the additional directions for a hymn to be sung before or after the post-Communion prayer (page 409) so it is not, strictly speaking, against rubrics. But once another hymn is added after the post-Communion prayer, whether processional or not, the Dismissal begins to get more distant from the communion of the people. Liturgical scholars are of mixed mind—or at least this one is—on how not to let the perfect be the enemy of the good in this case. If the processional hymn is placed immediately after the post-Communion prayer, and then the Dismissal follows, at least the Dismissal is the last thing that the congregation hears before they depart. But planning the processional hymn after the Dismissal (i.e., dismissing people from the "front" of the space), keeps the linkage between Communion and Dismissal. This is more a matter of planning than presiding, and planners will make their choice.

As to the post-Communion blessing: well aware that I will never win this battle, I nevertheless point out that a blessing by the priest—which is optional in Rite II—when measured against the fact that the people have just received the Body and Blood of the Lord, is arguably superfluous.

"Alleluias" are added to the Dismissal during Easter season. Alleluias are not added when it is not Easter season. The more of the prayer book's seasonal adjustments you make universal, the less the rhythm of the seasons is felt. While on the topic: add the Alleluias to the beginning of the Dismissal: "Alleluia, Alleluia, let us go forth in the name of Christ." Thus, our going is enfolded, beginning to end, by Alleluias.

7

Best Practices
for Baptism

aptism is, as the prayer book puts it, "full initiation by water and the Holy Spirit into Christ's Body, the Church."[1] Baptism is a double signifier: it is a celebration of grace freely given, and transformation fully entered. In Baptism we celebrate that we are beloved children of God; all is given. At the same time, we know that we have barely begun to be the children God has made us to be. Baptism holds these two together in a non-binary way: we celebrate the gift and are initiated into a long path of transformation. Baptism is not a pastoral rite, though it will have pastoral effects; and it is not a service provided to religious consumers, though it does respond to the conative dimensions of human life that candidates (even adult candidates) for Baptism cannot entirely name. It is an enactment of *initiation* into a material-spiritual community whose chief virtue is gratitude, from which certain other behaviors and patterns of life ensue, and for which strengthening and formation occur through the life of the crucified-risen One received at the Eucharistic Table, over and over again.

---

1. BCP, p. 298.

Fundamental Principles

Baptism best occurs on the Principal Feasts recommended by the prayer book. The 1979 prayer book indicates four occasions that are "most appropriate" for Baptism;[2] all are Major Feasts closely connected to the identity and mission of Christ. In a hermeneutical circle, keeping to these dates strengthens our sense of the significance of Baptism, and performing Baptism on those dates lifts up the significance of those days. (See the comment on "toggles" in the chapter on "General Principles and Best Practices.") At any rate, Baptism should almost never be done except on Sundays. The linkage between Baptism and the Sunday, Sunday and the Eucharist, along with the revised Proper Liturgies for Special Days are how the prayer book encodes the theology of the Paschal Mystery. Performing Baptism as a matter of convenience at other times erodes the paschal linkage of the performance and the meaning of Baptism as inextricably connected to the life of the assembly of disciples that celebrates Sunday in and Sunday out. There are those who will claim that aggregating baptisms on these four days (plus the bishop's visit) is an impracticality. I have served parishes with 8 people on a Sunday, and parishes with 800. It takes not much longer to do multiple water baths and anointings than it takes to do one; the service is not significantly lengthened by baptizing more candidates. (Is the length of the service our highest priority anyway?)

---

2. BCP, p. 312.

Bring the bishop—preferably the diocesan, or suffragan, or assisting bishop, or—in the case of the impossibility of doing so—whatever version of a bishop you can find that is approved by your diocesan!—to baptize adults. Having adults baptized by the bishop brings together several initiatory elements together in a single event. The candidates, in one ritual act, are initiated into the community that receives its Life as a gift, make a mature affirmation before the chief presider, teacher, and pastor of the assembly to respond to this gift with nothing less than all they are, and become baptized and confirmed communicants of the Episcopal Church in a single action. The Great Vigil of Easter and Pentecost are particularly appropriate days to do this, though any other time of the bishop's visitation is certainly fine, as that occasion will bear its own importance in the life of the local assembly.

The Rite

Baptismal candidates should be welcomed and celebrated. Pre-liturgy gatherings are fine. Removable Baptismal certificates on festal banners for the procession are fine. By all means, do these things and more. But... these ancillary festivities and symbols point to and do not supplant the centrality of water bath and chrismation, proclamation of the Word, and prayer. The rite should be performed in such a way that a sense of joyful *gravitas* is clearly communicated by these central actions, which should be clearly visible to all.

The presider presides at Baptism at the spot where she presides at other times for similar moments in liturgy. In general, there are a few places where presiders stand to lead liturgy: a chancel *prie-deux*, the broad step, the pavement, the chair, behind the Font or Altar, depending on the space. Multiplying these in a utilitarian way or doing a "one-off" for Baptism destabilizes the sacred geography of the assembly. There are other times than the Baptismal interrogation when the candidates or newly baptized can be invited to turn to face those gathered: the query to the people whether they will "support these persons in their new life in Christ," for example, or at the welcome of the newly baptized. Having the candidates face the people in the same direction as the presider is facing looks ridiculous and feels awkward to them. The candidates face the presider when the presider is querying them.

In most places where the font is not adjacent to the Altar space, the examination is best conducted from the "front" of the church, and a procession to the Font then occurs as the prayers for the candidates are offered. This is, of course, unless the Font is positioned at the "front" of the church, in which case everything occurs right there. The rite supports this movement nicely and economically: the Baptismal interrogation occurs, the presider and the candidates process to the Font during the prayers for the Candidates. In this sort of space, it is wise to have the presider lead the Candidates to the Font rather than take their usual place at the end of the procession; this puts the presider in position easily to slip behind the Font and face the people, and the Candidates then gather around, staggered to left or right so that the Font remains visible to all.

Water is poured directly, and simply, if noisily. There is absolutely no function or symbolic purpose to progressively raising the vessel as one pours the water into the Font. We are not hip waiters in the hottest restaurant, and who among us knows why they do that even there? The water might be poured by the deacon, in the preferable event that a deacon is present.

The structure of the Thanksgiving over the Water parallels the structure of the Great Thanksgiving of the Eucharist. Thus, the order is as follows: the water is poured, preparing the Font just as the Altar is prepared before the Eucharistic Prayer; then comes "The Lord be with you," followed on directly by the Thanksgiving over the Water, which is prayed in *orans*, until the time of the epiclesis comes and the presider touches the water. (Those administering the water: please consider the symbolic message in shaking the water from one's hands after the Baptismal epiclesis! If necessary and possible, a towel can be laid along the lip of the font upon which the presider can gently and without fanfare lay their hand as they move back to the *orans* to complete the prayer.)

The One from whom all life exists offers grace, love, and mercy *beyond measure*. The use and amount of water and Chrism should reflect this fact so far as possible. Hint: a teaspoon of water imposed on the Candidate, while valid, misses the mark here, as does a fingernail's worth of Chrism drawn from a tiny vessel attached to one's finger which, while keeping the vestment and vessel companies in business, is not even visible to the assembly and lacks the *gravitas* of the sign's holy referent.

Baptism is not a naming ceremony. The child has a perfectly good name given by the parents and duly recorded on the birth certificate. "Name this child" was *removed* from Baptismal rite in 1979 and is not to be confused with the rubric that the child is presented to the presider by name, which is pragmatic, not ritually enactive. (The reader who finds himself incredulous at this suggestion should lay the 1928 book and the 1979 book next to each other and compare the two!)

The best order for the core elements of the Baptismal rite: water bath, then chrismation, then post-Baptismal prayer. Some ancient rites evidenced several anointings along the way to the water bath and at least one evidenced two anointings after. In our current rite, the water bath and the handlaying with chrismation are the most powerful symbolic actions and central to the rite. The 1979 prayer book makes the chrismation optional—a product of its day in bringing chrismation back into Episcopal usage. Almost everywhere Chrism is now used, and appropriately so. The 1979 prayer book gives two options for the order of the chrismation and post-Baptismal prayer: either one can follow the water bath. *By far the best practice*— and let's hope a future authorized rite enshrines it—is that the bath and the chrismation belong together. The formulae uttered there are *performative* and rendered in the *present tense*. The post-Baptismal prayer, on the other hand, descending from earlier precedents one can research elsewhere, is *petitionary* and rendered in the *past tense*. For the rite's organization, it is most effective to say the post-Baptismal prayer after the water bath and chrismation have been done for all candidates.

By the measure, then, of symbolic rhetoric and practicality, bath-Chrism-prayer-welcome is the most defensible pattern.

If the font is away from the "front" of the church or wherever one normally presides, then return with the newly baptized after the chrismation, and receive and welcome the newly baptized there. One can move back on the *Vidi aquam* or some other appropriate music. This way of staging the movement "resets" the liturgy to proceed as normal from where it is usually led, and—as a practicality—is far easier than saying the Welcome and Peace from the Font and then having to navigate the aisle through a swarm of peace-making Christians to get back to one's normal place of presiding.

Prayers of the People are an essential element of the *ordo* and should always be included in our major public liturgies, including Baptism. This is often overlooked in Episcopal services, and most unfortunately so. *What moment could be more important for the assembly to offer Intercessions for the world than when new candidates have just been welcomed to "share with us in [Christ's] eternal priesthood?"*[3] (The Prayers for the Candidates, offered before the Thanksgiving over the Water, are not full intercessions for the world.) The Prayers of the People on a Baptismal day either follow the Peace and lead into the Offertory; or, the service might continue with the Offertory and the use of Eucharistic Prayer D, in which the Intercessions can be appropriately placed.

---

3. BCP, p. 308.

The presentation of the newly baptized into the community and their reception by the community is a liturgical act and should place as much celebratory weight on the adults as on the children or infants. Consider carefully whether the "baby parade" down the aisle at the Peace serves this purpose, or some other.

At Baptism, the lections, the vesture, and the ceremonial actions link the Baptismal action to the ordo of time. Use the lections appointed for the day. (The Baptismal propers in the 1979 prayer book[4] are intended for a case in which Baptism does not occur on a Sunday. If on a Sunday—preferably on the recommended days—the propers for that day are used. The Baptismal propers *can* be substituted during Ordinary time.) Dress the church and the ministers in the liturgical color of the day. If the local practice is to use incense, the Font should be censed as well as the Altar. Censing of the Font occurs immediately after the water is poured, just as, in the Eucharist, the censing occurs immediately after the altar is prepared.

The Episcopal Church encourages the Communion of children who are baptized. At the very least, in cases where the parents really want the child to defer, infants (with a drop of wine placed to the lips) and children should be communicated on their Baptismal day, notwithstanding the clarity or confusion that reigns in the parish about the theology and practice of Confirmation. Much work remains to be done there and goes well beyond this book.

---

4. BCP, p. 928.

The Paschal Candle is placed in a spot located near the Font on Baptismal days, and lit on those days. This should also occur during Baptismal days when there is no Baptism, at which time the rite should ALWAYS include the renewal of Baptismal vows. Where space is problematic, the Candle might be placed near the Ambo or Altar, as the giving of light lit from the Paschal Candle is nice but entirely optional. Note: the Paschal Candle also stays out for the *entire* Great Fifty Days of Easter—*through and including* Pentecost, as specified by the prayer book. The candle does not "disappear" on Ascension Day, because Jesus, like Elvis, has left the building. Please let this practice die. Allegory quickly becomes playacting of the past; and this distances the assembly from the liturgical action as concerning, precisely, the *present life of the assembly* through its participation in the living Christ who is, by virtue of the Ascension, absent from one particular place and so present in every place.

Conclusion

The Presider's Art

At many points throughout this work, in the course of reflection on the nature of liturgy, general principles, or at particular points of best practice, I have touched on one or another recommendation for the presider's *conduct* of the rite. It seems fitting to conclude this inquiry with a few *summary* comments on this matter—about the presider's bearing, movement, speech, and presence in any liturgical setting—including some thoughts about personal distinctives and cultural norms that shape the presider's art.

A good way of thinking about the presider's conduct is through the notion of the Aristotelian mean. Aristotle's notion of the mean as a measure of behavior was always the point between two extremes, which themselves would be appropriate to the context. For example, bravery would be the mean between cowardly withdrawal and reckless approach, but what might count as bravery in one situation might not in another.[1] This way of thinking about ritual presence in the work of presiding is useful because it honors not only the general principles applied, but the style and persona of the person who applies them and the context in which they are applied.

Along this line, we might first say the following overall about the presider's bearing, movement, and presence.

---

1. "Aristotle's Ethics," Section 5.1, https://plato.stanford.edu/entries/aristotle-ethics/#DoctMean

The presider needs to take herself very seriously and not too seriously at all! The assembly takes its cues from the presider's leadership, but that leadership serves, not the presider's importance, but the assembly's worship. As a presider, one wants to be far enough "forward" to lead the liturgy along, but far enough "back" to sense the Spirit at work in the assembly, to let its praise and prayer be felt as corporate and alive, and to make space for the other ministers who lead various parts of the liturgy under the presider's guiding oversight.

The bearing of the presider is never casual, but never stiff. The presider should be steady, present, and non-anxious. Movements are economical. Various extraneous movements of the hands or feet, restless turning of the body in the presider's chair, and the like, should be avoided. Gracious, purposeful movement that serve the actions of the liturgy are the aim. Movements that are too fast seem instrumental; too slow, and they make the movement itself the point—which is decidedly not the point. Bodily gestures made *toward* the assembly—for example, a gesture of invitation—are made with confident clarity—half-gestures subtly convey a lack of confidence or uncertainty about what is happening. Movements across or around the space follow clean lines of approach; corners are turned, not with a military crispness, but neither do we meander around them as if we don't know where we are going. In speech, one is neither too fast, suggesting a lack of importance around what is happening, nor too slow, which becomes ponderous and distracting. We speak of holy things, and we handle holy things, and we do so with a bearing appropriate to that reality.

In sum, when standing, one is steady; when seated, one is steady; in one's movement and bearing and speech, one is purposeful and steady. There is a sense of solemnity in all these dimensions of the presider's work that aim for a "golden mean" that lives, not simply between gravitas and joy, but enfolds them both.

Lest one imagine there is a perfect, single target that every presider aims for in all these things, one particular style between the extremes that is *right*, it is important to note that particular presiders embody this kind of presence and bearing differently. While the target we aim for, the mean we seek, is not infinitely varied, it will be different for each of us. Our bodies, our personal characteristics, our ways of being with and for others will play into how we preside. When I aim in my action toward solemnity, it will look different when another presider does so, and different still from a third. The mean between extremes that we presiders aim for will be the mean as we embody it, in our individuality.

Furthermore, there will often be characteristic differences between, say, a funeral in New Orleans and a funeral in Portland, Maine, between a "charismatic" Eucharist and an "Anglo-Catholic" one, between a Sunday morning liturgy in Cape Town and one in Dodoma, Osaka, Paris, Oslo, Lisbon, Quito, Atlanta, or Vancouver, or among the several liturgies on a given Sunday across any one of those cities! These will often mean different styles of presiding. Culture, race, and ethnicity will also affect the *mean* that the presider aims for in her leadership. African, Asian, Hispanic, Anglo; styles of liturgy vary across culture and race and ethnicity and at the same time one cannot, for a moment, be sure that two assemblies of similar predominant ethnicity or race will do liturgy that is similar—and even then, most assemblies are not monochromatic! The rite may be the same; the performance will likely be at least a little different. We must say then, of our steadiness as presiders, of our gravitas and joy—of our cultivated presence as "strong, loving and wise," as Robert Hovda once put it[2]—that we may also be called upon to be steady in exuberance and steady in our reserve, strong in our weeping and strong in our dancing! The mean toward which we aim in liturgical leadership will be shaped not only by the nature of ritual and its enactment, but by who we are, by our own walk in Christ, and by the makeup and style of the assembly we serve.

————————————

There is so much more than can be said of good practices in curating, planning, and presiding. What I have said here is neither the first nor final word. What is offered here reflects my own thirty-three years of presiding, my successes and mistakes, my experience as a member of many liturgical assemblies, my sense of common missteps that I see as I travel around the churches, and of course, my scholarship and teaching in these matters. Where the reader has found my comments commend-able or even obvious, I hope that means it is because my reason-ing is sound and my observations helpful. Where the reader has disagreed, I hope that they grant that my recommendations are not *just* an expression of personal preference but rooted in ritual theory, liturgical theology, and theories of practice, *and* that they will feel empowered to develop their own thoughtful defense of their practices.

————————————

2. Robert Hovda, *Strong, Loving, and Wise: Presiding in Liturgy*, 5th ed. (Collegeville: Liturgical Press, 1981).

There is nothing so powerful as liturgy done well and beautifully, granting us a partial sense of the world's redemption and transfiguration at which God in Christ is ever at work through the Holy Spirit. The privilege of gathering the people of God around Book and Font and Table to participate through praise and prayer in that divine mission is at once a great source of joy and a call to deep humility. May God grant to us all, by divine mercy and grace, that the life we enact in our liturgical gathering, we also enact day by day, to the glory of the God who redeems us all.

Appendix A

Further Reading
in Ritual Theory

For readers who would like to know more about the
ritual theory that informs this book, I offer the following. Generally, liturgists who pay attention to ritual
theory (oddly, not all do, but that is a longer story!) will look
to the classic work of Durkheim, Geertz, van Gennep, and
Victor Turner, and in the modern period to a company that
includes Ronald Grimes and Catherine Bell. The works of
these authors are classics for a reason, and Grimes and Bell
have certainly been prolific and helpful. They are well worth
investigation and the motivated reader can find their work in
various editions with a search of any relevant database.

While Grimes and Bell have been helpful to my own work,
I have learned a great deal more from Jonathan Z. Smith and,
most powerfully, from Roy Rappaport, whose masterful work
on ritual theory would have been further elaborated, had he
not left us too soon. For anyone who wants to dig into one
comprehensive if not entirely finished theory on ritual that
captures how ritualization enacts a lifeworld, Rappaport's book
is the one I would recommend:

Smith, Jonathan Z. *To Take Place: Toward Theory in Ritual.* Chicago:
University of Chicago Press, 1992.
Rappaport, Roy A. *Ritual and Religion in the Making of Humanity.*
Cambridge: Cambridge University Press, 1999.

Another book, quite fascinating in its thinking with the classics, like Geertz, but correcting and modifying some of his presumptions, is the following:

> Seligman, Adam B., et al. *Ritual and its Consequences: An Essay on the Limits of Sincerity.* Oxford: Oxford University Press, 2008.

Of particular interest in this book is a chapter contributed by Michael Puett entitled "Ritual and the Subjunctive." His consideration of the way participants in ritual know that the world they are enacting is not the world that they live in has fruitful implications for Christians who want to understand liturgy fundamentally as an *eschatological* performance. (On the theological front, in regard to this approach to liturgical theology, see Don E. Saliers, *Worship as Theology: Foretaste of Glory Divine*, cited in the text of this book.)

In addition to these important works, there has been some interest in ritual among philosophers of religion. A collection of insightful essays to which I have turned again and again in recent years is the following book, with an astute *double-entendre* for a title:

> Schilbrack, Kevin, ed. *Thinking Through Rituals: Philosophical Perspectives.* New York: Routledge, 2004.

Particularly provocative essays in the book include those by the author himself and by Nick Crossley, Michael Raposa, and Steven Kepnes.

There is an entire literature on these matters, but for starters I commend these texts to the reader who wants to go deeper in these matters.

Appendix B

Holy Eucharist Rite II
Prayer C (two forms)

As approved for trial use by General Convention 2022 with referral to the Standing Committee on Liturgy and Music to develop a method of evaluation Eucharistic Prayer C – 1979 Prayer Book Updated

In this prayer, the lines in italics are spoken by the People.
The Celebrant, whether bishop or priest,
faces them and sings or says

[May] God be with you.

And also with you.

Lift up your hearts.

We lift them to the Lord.

Let us give thanks to the Lord our God.

It is right to give our thanks and praise.

Then, facing the Holy Table, the Celebrant proceeds

God of all power, Source and Sustainer of the Universe, you are worthy of glory and praise.

Glory to you for ever and ever.

At your command all things came to be: shining light and enfolding dark; the vast expanse of interstellar space, galaxies, suns, and this fragile earth, our island home.

By your will they were created and have their being.

From the primal elements you brought forth the human race, and blessed us with memory, reason, and skill. You made us the stewards of your creation. But we turned against you, and betrayed your trust; and we turned against one another.

Have mercy, Lord, for we are sinners in your sight.

Again and again, you called us to return. Through prophets and sages you revealed your righteous Law. And in the fullness of time you sent your eternal Word, born of your servant Mary, to fulfill your Law, opening for us the way of freedom and peace.

By his blood, he reconciled us.
By his wounds, we are healed.

And therefore we praise you, joining with the heavenly chorus, with prophets, apostles, and martyrs, and with all those in every generation who have looked to you in hope, to proclaim with them your glory, in their unending hymn:

Celebrant and People

Holy, holy, holy Lord, God of power and might, heaven and earth are full of your glory.

Hosanna in the highest.

Blessed is the one who comes in the name of the Lord.

Hosanna in the highest.

The Celebrant continues
At the following words concerning the bread, the Celebrant
is to hold it, or lay a hand upon it; and at the words
concerning the cup, to hold or place a hand upon the cup
and any other vessel containing wine to be consecrated.

On the night he was betrayed Jesus took bread, said the blessing, broke the bread, and gave it to his friends, and said, "Take,
eat: This is my Body, which is given for you. Do this for the
remembrance of me."
After supper, Jesus took the cup of wine, gave thanks, and said,
"Drink this, all of you: This is my Blood of the new Covenant,
which is shed for you and for all for the forgiveness of sins.
Whenever you drink it, do this for the remembrance of me.'"
Remembering now his work of redemption and offering to you
this sacrifice of thanksgiving,

We celebrate Christ's death and resurrection as we await the day
of his coming.

Therefore, O God, we who have been redeemed by Jesus
Christ, and made a new people by water and the Spirit, now
bring before you these gifts. Sanctify them by your Holy Spirit
to be the Body and Blood of Jesus Christ our Savior. Sanctify
us also, and let the grace of this Holy Communion make us
one body, one spirit in Christ, that we may worthily serve the
world in his name.

Risen Lord, be known to us in the breaking of the Bread.

God of our ancestors; Redeemer and Mother of Israel; God
and Father of our Lord Jesus Christ: Open our eyes to see
your hand at work in the world about us. Deliver us from the

presumption of coming to this Table for solace only and not for strength; for pardon only and not for renewal.

Accept these prayers and praises, Almighty God, through Jesus Christ our great High Priest, to whom, with you and the Holy Spirit, your Church gives honor, glory, and worship, from generation to generation. *AMEN.*

Continue with the Lord's Prayer on p. 364

Eucharistic Prayer C – Fixed Responses (with rubrics)

In this prayer, the lines in italics are spoken by the People.
The Celebrant, whether bishop or priest,
faces them and sings or says

The Lord be with you. *or* God be with you.

And also with you.

Lift up your hearts.

We lift them to the Lord.

Let us give thanks to the Lord our God.

It is right to give our thanks and praise.

Then facing the Holy Table, the Celebrant proceeds

It is right to give you thanks and praise, O Lord, our God, sustainer of the universe.

Glory to you for ever and ever.

At your command all things came to be: shining light and enfolding dark; the vast expanse of interstellar space, galaxies, suns, the planets in their courses, and this fragile earth, our island home; by your will they were created and have their being. From the primal elements you brought forth the human race, and blessed us with memory, reason, and skill; you made us the stewards of creation.

Glory to you for ever and ever.

But we turned against you, and betrayed your trust; and we turned against one another. Again and again you called us to return. Through prophets and sages you revealed your righteous law. In the fullness of time you sent your Son, born of a woman, to be our Savior. He was wounded for our transgressions, and bruised for our iniquities. By his death he opened to us the way of freedom and peace.

Glory to you for ever and ever.

Therefore we praise you, joining with the heavenly chorus, with prophets, apostles, and martyrs, and with those in every generation who have looked to you in hope, to proclaim with them your glory, in their unending hymn:

Celebrant and People

Holy, holy, holy Lord, God of power and might, heaven and earth are full of your glory.

Hosanna in the highest.

Blessed is the one who comes in the name of the Lord.

Hosanna in the highest.

The people stand or kneel.
At the following words concerning the bread, the Celebrant
is to hold it, or lay a hand upon it; and at the words

*concerning the cup, to hold or place a hand upon the cup
and any other vessel containing wine to be consecrated.*

Blessed are you, Lord our God, for sending us Jesus, the Christ,
who on the night he was handed over to suffering and death,
took bread, said the blessing, broke the bread, gave it to his
friends, and said, "Take, eat: this is my body which is given for
you. Do this for the remembrance of me."

In the same way, after supper, he took the cup of wine; he
gave you thanks, and said, "Drink this, all of you: this is my
blood of the new covenant, which is shed for you and for all
for the forgiveness of sins. Whenever you drink it, do this for
the remembrance of me."

Remembering now his work of redemption, and offering to
you this sacrifice of thanksgiving, we celebrate his death and
resurrection, as we await the day of his coming.

Glory to you for ever and ever.

Therefore, we who have been redeemed by Jesus Christ, and
made a new people by water and the Spirit, now bring before
you these gifts. Sanctify them by your Holy Spirit to be the
Body and Blood of Jesus Christ our Savior. Sanctify us also,
and let the grace of this Holy Communion make us one body,
one spirit in Christ, that we may worthily serve the world in
his name.

Glory to you for ever and ever.

Pour out your Spirit upon the whole earth and make it your
new creation.

Gather your Church together from the ends of the earth into
your kingdom, where peace and justice are revealed, that we,

with all your people, of every language, race, and nation, may share the banquet you have promised.

Through Christ, with Christ, and in Christ, all honor and glory are yours, creator of all.

Glory to you for ever and ever. AMEN.

Continue with the Lord's Prayer on p. 364

Appendix C

The Holy Eucharist Rite II
(Expansive Language),
approved for trial use
by General Convention 2018

The Word of God

A hymn, psalm, or anthem may be sung.
The people standing, the Celebrant says

> Blessed be God: *most* holy, glorious, and undivided Trinity.

or Blessed be God: Father, Son, and Holy Spirit.

People And blessed be God's reign, now and for ever. Amen.

In place of the above, from Easter Day
through the Day of Pentecost

Alleluia. Christ is risen.

People Christ is risen indeed. Alleluia.

In Lent and on other penitential occasions

> Blessed be God who forgives all our sins.

People God's mercy endures for ever.

The Celebrant may say:

> Almighty God, to you all hearts are open, all desires

known, and from you no secrets are hid: Cleanse the thoughts of our hearts by the inspiration of your Holy Spirit, that we may perfectly love you, and worthily magnify your holy Name; through Christ our Lord. *Amen.*

The rubrics of the Prayer Book (p. 356) provide that when appointed, the Gloria in excelsis or "some other song of praise" may be used. Supplemental canticles (Enriching our Worship 1, pp. 25-41) or canticles from the Book of Common Prayer (pp. 85-96) are among the appropriate alternatives. On other occasions the following is used

Lord, have mercy.

Christ, have mercy.

Lord, have mercy

or this

Kyrie eleison.

Christe eleison.

Kyrie eleison.

or this

Holy God,
Holy and Mighty,
Holy Immortal One,
Have mercy upon us.

The Collect of the Day

The Celebrant says to the people

> God be with you. or The Lord be with you.

People And also with you.

> Let us pray.

The Celebrant says the Collect.

People Amen.

The Lessons

The people sit. One or two Lessons, as appointed, are read, the Reader first saying

> A Reading (Lesson) from _____ .

A citation giving chapter and verse may be added. After each Reading, the Reader may say

> The Word of the Lord.

or

> Hear what the Spirit is saying to God's people.

or

> Hear what the Spirit is saying to the Churches.

People Thanks be to God.

or the Reader may say

> Here ends the Reading (Epistle).

Silence may follow.
A psalm, hymn, or anthem may follow each Reading.
Then, all standing, the Deacon or a Priest
reads the Gospel, first saying

> The Holy Gospel of our Savior Jesus Christ according
> to _____ .

People Glory to you, Lord Christ.

After the Gospel, the Reader says

> The Gospel of our Savior.

People Praise to you, Lord Christ.

The Sermon

On Sundays and other Major Feasts there follows, all standing

The Nicene Creed

We believe in one God,
> the Father, the Almighty,
> maker of heaven and earth,
> of all that is, seen and unseen.

We believe in one Lord, Jesus Christ,
> the only Son of God,
> eternally begotten of the Father,
> God from God, Light from Light,
> true God from true God, begotten, not made,
> of one Being with the Father;
> through him all things were made.

For us and for our salvation
> he came down from heaven,

was incarnate of the Holy Spirit and the Virgin Mary
and became truly human.
For our sake he was crucified under Pontius Pilate;
he suffered death and was buried.
On the third day he rose again
in accordance with the Scriptures;
he ascended into heaven
and is seated at the right hand of the Father.
He will come again in glory to judge the living and
the dead,
and his kingdom will have no end.
We believe in the Holy Spirit, the Lord, the giver of life,
who proceeds from the Father,
who with the Father and the Son is worshiped and
glorified,
who has spoken through the prophets.
We believe in one holy catholic and apostolic Church.
We acknowledge one baptism for the forgiveness of
sins.
We look for the resurrection of the dead,
and the life of the world to come. Amen.

The Prayers of the People

Prayer is offered with intercession for
The Universal Church, its members, and its mission
The Nation and all in authority
The welfare of the world
The concerns of the local community
Those who suffer and those in any trouble

The departed (with commemoration of a saint when appropriate)
See the forms beginning on Book of Common Prayer, page
383, and the additional rubrics concerning the Prayers of
the People found in Enriching Our Worship 1, pages 54–55.
If there is no celebration of the Communion, or if a priest
is not available, the service is concluded as indicated in the
Additional Directions of the Book of Common Prayer.

Confession of Sin

A Confession of Sin is said here if it has not been said
earlier. On occasion, the Confession may be omitted.
One of the sentences from the Penitential Order
or Enriching Our Worship 1 may be said.
The Deacon or Celebrant says

Let us confess our sins against God and our neighbor.

Silence may be kept.
Minister and People

Most merciful God,
we confess that we have sinned against you
in thought, word, and deed,
by what we have done,
and by what we have left undone.
We have not loved you with our whole heart;
we have not loved our neighbors as ourselves.
We are truly sorry and we humbly repent.
For the sake of our Savior Jesus Christ,
have mercy on us and forgive us;
that we may delight in your will,

and walk in your ways,
to the glory of your Name. Amen.

The Bishop when present, or the Priest, stands and says

Almighty God have mercy on you, forgive you all your sins
through the grace of Jesus Christ, strengthen you in all goodness, and by the power of the Holy Spirit keep you in eternal
life. Amen.

The Peace

All stand. The Celebrant says to the people

> The peace of Christ be always with you.

People   And also with you.

*Then the Ministers and People may greet one
another in the name of Jesus Christ.*

The Holy Communion

*The Celebrant may begin the Offertory with one of the
sentences provided, or with some other sentence of Scripture.
During the Offertory, a hymn, psalm, or anthem may be sung.
Representatives of the congregation bring the people's
offerings of bread and wine, and money or other gifts,
to the deacon or celebrant. The people stand while the
offerings are presented and placed on the Altar.*

The Great Thanksgiving

Alternative forms will be found on page 367 and following.

Eucharistic Prayer A

The people remain standing. The Celebrant, whether bishop or priest, faces them and sings or says

Celebrant The Lord be with you. *or* God be with you.

People And also with you.

Celebrant Lift up your hearts.

People We lift them to the Lord.

Celebrant Let us give thanks to the Lord our God.

People It is right to give our thanks and praise.

Then, facing the Holy Table, the Celebrant proceeds

It is right, and a good and joyful thing, always and everywhere to give thanks to you, Almighty God, Creator of heaven and earth.

Here a Proper Preface is sung or said on all Sundays, and on other occasions as appointed.

Therefore we praise you, joining our voices with Angels and Archangels and with all the company of heaven, who for ever sing this hymn to proclaim the glory of your Name:

Celebrant and People

Holy, holy, holy Lord, God of power and might,
heaven and earth are full of your glory.

Hosanna in the highest.

Blessed is the one who comes in the name of the Lord.

Hosanna in the highest.

The people stand or kneel. Then the Celebrant continues

Holy and gracious God: In your infinite love you made us for yourself; and, when we had fallen into sin and become subject to evil and death, you, in your mercy, sent Jesus Christ, your only and eternal Son, to share our human nature, to live and die as one of us, to reconcile us to you, the God and maker of all.

Jesus stretched out his arms upon the cross, and offered himself in obedience to your will, a perfect sacrifice for the whole world.

At the following words concerning the bread, the Celebrant is to hold it or lay a hand upon it; and at the words concerning the cup, to hold or place a hand upon the cup and any other vessel containing wine to be consecrated.

On the night he was handed over to suffering and death, our Savior Jesus Christ took bread; and when he had given thanks to you, he broke it, and gave it to his disciples, and said, "Take, eat: This is my Body, which is given for you. Do this for the remembrance of me."

After supper Jesus took the cup of wine; and when he had given thanks, he gave it to them, and said, "Drink this, all of you: This is my Blood of the new Covenant, which is shed for you and for many for the forgiveness of sins. Whenever you drink it, do this for the remembrance of me."

Therefore we proclaim the mystery of faith:

Celebrant and People

Christ has died.
Christ is risen.
Christ will come again.

The Celebrant continues

We celebrate the memorial of our redemption, Almighty God, in this sacrifice of praise and thanksgiving. Recalling Christ's death, resurrection, and ascension, we offer you these gifts. Sanctify them by your Holy Spirit to be for your people the Body and Blood of your Son, the holy food and drink of new and unending life in Christ. Sanctify us also that we may faithfully receive this holy Sacrament, and serve you in unity, constancy, and peace; and at the last day bring us with all your saints into the joy of your eternal kingdom.
All this we ask through Jesus Christ our Savior. By Christ, and with Christ, and in Christ, in the unity of the Holy Spirit all honor and glory is yours, Almighty God, now and for ever. *AMEN.*
And now, as our Savior Christ has taught us, we are bold to say,

People and Celebrant

Our Father, who art in heaven,
   hallowed be thy Name,
   thy kingdom come,
   thy will be done,
      on earth as it is in heaven.
Give us this day our daily bread.
And forgive us our trespasses,

as we forgive those
who trespass against us.
And lead us not into temptation,
but deliver us from evil.
For thine is the kingdom,
and the power, and the glory,
for ever and ever. Amen.

Or this

As our Savior Christ has taught us, we now pray,

People and Celebrant

Our Father in heaven,
hallowed be your Name,
your kingdom come,
your will be done,
on earth as in heaven.
Give us today our daily bread.
Forgive us our sins
as we forgive those
who sin against us.
Save us from the time of trial,
and deliver us from evil.
For the kingdom, the power,
and the glory are yours,
now and for ever. Amen.

The Breaking of the Bread

The Celebrant breaks the consecrated Bread.
A period of silence is kept.
Then may be sung or said

[Alleluia.] Christ our Passover is sacrificed for us;

Therefore let us keep the feast. [Alleluia.]
In Lent, Alleluia is omitted, and may be omitted
at other times except during Easter Season.
In place of, or in addition to, the preceding,
some other suitable anthem may be used.
Facing the people, the Celebrant says the
following Invitation or similar words.

The Gifts of God for the People of God.

and may add   Take them in remembrance that Christ died
for you, and feed on him in your hearts by
faith, with thanksgiving.

The ministers receive the Sacrament in both kinds,
and then immediately deliver it to the people.
The Bread and the Cup are given to the
communicants with these words

The Body (Blood) of our Lord Jesus Christ keep you in everlasting life. [*Amen.*]

or with these words

The Body of Christ, the bread of heaven. [*Amen.*]
The Blood of Christ, the cup of salvation. [*Amen.*]

During the ministration of Communion,
hymns, psalms, or anthems may be sung.
When necessary, the Celebrant consecrates additional
bread and wine, using the provided form in the
Additional Directions of the Book of Common Prayer.
After Communion, the Celebrant says

Let us pray.

Celebrant and People

Eternal God,
you have graciously accepted us as living members
of our Savior Jesus Christ,
and you have fed us with spiritual food
in the Sacrament of his Body and Blood.
Send us now into the world in peace,
and grant us strength and courage
to love and serve you
with gladness and singleness of heart; through Christ our
Savior. Amen.

or the following

Almighty and ever living God,
we thank you for feeding us with the spiritual food
of the most precious Body and Blood
of your Son our Savior Jesus Christ;
and for assuring us in these holy mysteries
that we are living members of the Body of your Christ,
and heirs of your eternal kingdom. And now, send us out
to do the work you have given us to do,

to love and serve you as faithful witnesses of Christ our Savior.
To him, to you, and to the Holy Spirit,
be honor and glory, now and for ever. Amen.

The Bishop when present, or the Priest, may bless the people.
The Deacon, or the Celebrant, dismisses them with these words

         Let us go forth in the name of Christ.

People   Thanks be to God.

or this

Deacon Go in peace to love and serve Jesus Christ our Savior.

People   Thanks be to God.

or this

Deacon Let us go forth into the world, rejoicing in the power
         of the Spirit.

People   Thanks be to God.

or this

Deacon Let us bless the Lord.

People   Thanks be to God.

From the Easter Vigil through the Day of Pentecost
"Alleluia, alleluia" is added to any of the dismissals.

Alternative Forms of the Great Thanksgiving

Eucharistic Prayer B

The people remain standing. The Celebrant,
whether bishop or priest, faces them and sings or says

	The Lord be with you. *or* God be with you.
People	And also with you.
Celebrant	Lift up your hearts.
People	We lift them to the Lord.
Celebrant	Let us give thanks to the Lord our God.
People	It is right to give our thanks and praise.

Then, facing the Holy Table, the Celebrant proceeds

It is right, and a good and joyful thing, always and everywhere to give thanks to you, Almighty God, Creator of heaven and earth.

Here a Proper Preface is sung or said on all
Sundays, and on other occasions as appointed.

Therefore we praise you, joining our voices with Angels and Archangels and with all the company of heaven, who for ever sing this hymn to proclaim the glory of your Name:

Celebrant and People

Holy, holy, holy Lord, God of power and might,
heaven and earth are full of your glory.

Hosanna in the highest.

Blessed is the one who comes in the name of the Lord.

Hosanna in the highest.

The people stand or kneel. Then the Celebrant continues

We give thanks to you, O God, for the goodness and love which you have made known to us in creation; in the calling of Israel to be your people; in your Word spoken through the prophets; and above all in Jesus Christ, the Word made flesh. For in these last days you sent Jesus to be incarnate from the Virgin Mary, to be the Savior and Redeemer of the world. In Christ, you have delivered us from evil, and made us worthy to stand before you. In Christ, you have brought us out of error into truth, out of sin into righteousness, out of death into life.

At the following words concerning the bread, the Celebrant is to hold it or lay a hand upon it; and at the words concerning the cup, to hold or place a hand upon the cup and any other vessel containing wine to be consecrated.

On the night before he died for us, our Savior Jesus Christ took bread; and when he had given thanks to you, he broke it, and gave it to his disciples, and said, "Take, eat: This is my Body, which is given for you. Do this for the remembrance of me."

After supper Jesus took the cup of wine; and when he had given thanks, he gave it to them, and said, "Drink this, all of you: This is my Blood of the new Covenant, which is shed for you and for many for the forgiveness of sins. Whenever you drink it, do this for the remembrance of me."

Therefore, according to his command, O Father,

Celebrant and People

We remember Christ's death,
We proclaim Christ's resurrection,
We await Christ's coming in glory;

The Celebrant continues

And we offer our sacrifice of praise and thanksgiving to you,
O Savior of all; presenting to you, from your creation, this
bread and this wine.

We pray you, gracious God, to send your Holy Spirit upon
these gifts that they may be the Sacrament of the Body of
Christ and his Blood of the new Covenant. Unite us in the
sacrifice of Jesus Christ, through whom we are acceptable to
you, being sanctified by the Holy Spirit. In the fullness of
time, put all things in subjection under your Christ, and bring
us to that heavenly country where, with [_____ and] all
your saints, we may enter the everlasting heritage of your
children; through Jesus Christ our Savior, the firstborn of
all creation, the head of the Church, and the author of our
salvation.

By Christ, and with Christ, and in Christ, in the unity of the
Holy Spirit all honor and glory is yours, Almighty God, now
and for ever. *AMEN.*

Continue with the Lord's Prayer on page 364.

Eucharistic Prayer D

The people remain standing. The Celebrant,
whether bishop or priest, faces them and sings or says

The Lord be with you. *or* God be with you.

People And also with you.

Celebrant Lift up your hearts.

People We lift them to the Lord.

Celebrant Let us give thanks to the Lord our God.

People It is right to give our thanks and praise.

Then, facing the Holy Table, the Celebrant proceeds

It is truly right to glorify you, Holy One, and to give you thanks; for you alone are God, living and true, dwelling in light inaccessible from before time and for ever. Fountain of life and source of all goodness, you made all things and fill them with your blessing; you created them to rejoice in the splendor of your radiance. Countless throngs of angels stand before you to serve you night and day; and, beholding the glory of your presence, they offer you unceasing praise. Joining with them, and giving voice to every creature under heaven, we acclaim you, and glorify your Name, as we sing (say),

Celebrant and People

Holy, holy, holy Lord, God of power and might,
heaven and earth are full of your glory.

Hosanna in the highest.

Blessed is the one who comes in the name of the Lord.

Hosanna in the highest.

The people stand or kneel.
Then the Celebrant continues

We acclaim you, holy God, glorious in power. Your mighty works reveal your wisdom and love. You formed us in your own image, giving the whole world into our care, so that, in obedience to you, our Creator, we might rule and serve all your creatures. When our disobedience took us far from you, you did not abandon us to the power of death. In your mercy you came to our help, so that in seeking you we might find you. Again and again you called us into covenant with you, and through the prophets you taught us to hope for salvation.

Holy God, you loved the world so much that in the fullness of time you sent your only Son to be our Savior. Incarnate by the Holy Spirit, born of the Virgin Mary, Jesus lived as one of us, yet without sin. To the poor he proclaimed the good news of salvation; to prisoners, freedom; to the sorrowful, joy. To fulfill your purpose Jesus gave himself up to death; and, rising from the grave, destroyed death, and made the whole creation new.

And that we might live no longer for ourselves, but for Christ who died and rose for us, you sent the Holy Spirit, your own first gift for those who believe, to complete your work in the world, and to bring to fulfillment the sanctification of all.

At the following words concerning the bread, the Celebrant
is to hold it or lay a hand upon it; and at the words

*concerning the cup, to hold or place a hand upon the cup
and any other vessel containing wine to be consecrated.*

When the hour had come for Jesus to be glorified by you, his heavenly Father, having loved his own who were in the world, he loved them to the end; at supper with them Jesus took bread, and when he had given thanks to you, he broke it, and gave it to his disciples, and said, "Take, eat: This is my Body, which is given for you. Do this for the remembrance of me."

After supper Jesus took the cup of wine; and when he had given thanks, he gave it to them, and said, "Drink this, all of you. This is my Blood of the new Covenant, which is shed for you and for many for the forgiveness of sins. Whenever you drink it, do this for the remembrance of me."

Almighty God, we now celebrate this memorial of our redemption. Recalling Christ's death and descent among the dead, proclaiming Christ's resurrection and ascension to your right hand, awaiting Christ's coming in glory; and offering to you, from the gifts you have given us, this bread and this cup, we praise you and we bless you.

Celebrant and People

We praise you, we bless you,
we give thanks to you,
and we pray to you, Lord our God.

The Celebrant continues

God our Creator, we pray that in your goodness and mercy your Holy Spirit may descend upon us, and upon these gifts, sanctifying them and showing them to be holy gifts for your holy people, the bread of life and the cup of salvation, the Body and Blood of our Savior Jesus Christ.

Grant that all who share this bread and cup may become one body and one spirit, a living sacrifice in Christ, to the praise of your Name.

Remember, Lord, your one holy catholic and apostolic Church, redeemed by the blood of your Christ. Reveal its unity, guard its faith, and preserve it in peace.

[Remember (NN. and) all who minister in your Church.]

[Remember all your people, and those who seek your truth.]

[Remember _____.]

[Remember all who have died in the peace of Christ, and those whose faith is known to you alone; bring them into the place of eternal joy and light.]

And grant that we may find our inheritance with [the Blessed Virgin Mary, with matriarchs, patriarchs, prophets, apostles, and martyrs, (with _____) and] all the saints who have found favor with you in ages past. We praise you in union with them and give you glory through Jesus Christ our Savior. Through Christ, and with Christ, and in Christ, all honor and glory are yours, Almighty God and Father, in the unity of the Holy Spirit, for ever and ever. *AMEN.*

Continue with the Lord's Prayer on page 364.

Proper Prefaces

Preface of the Lord's Day

To be used on Sundays as appointed,
but not on the succeeding weekdays

1. Of God the Father

For you are the source of light and life; you made us in your image, and called us to new life in Jesus Christ our Lord.

or this

2. Of God the Son

Through Jesus Christ our Lord; who on the first day of the week overcame death and the grave, and by his glorious resurrection opened to us the way of everlasting life.

or the following

3. Of God the Holy Spirit

For by water and the Holy Spirit you have made us a new people in Jesus Christ our Lord, to show forth your glory in all the world.

Prefaces for Seasons

To be used on Sundays and weekdays alike, except as otherwise appointed for Holy Days and Various Occasions

Advent

Because you sent your beloved Son to redeem us from sin and death, and to make us heirs of everlasting life; that when Christ shall come again in power and great triumph to judge the world, we may without shame or fear rejoice to behold his appearing.

Incarnation

Because you gave Jesus Christ, your only Son, to be born for us; who, by the mighty power of the Holy Spirit, was made perfectly human of the flesh of the Virgin Mary his mother; so that we might be delivered from the bondage of sin, and receive power to become your children.

Epiphany

Because in the mystery of the Word made flesh, you have caused a new light to shine in our hearts, to give the knowledge of your glory in the face of your Son Jesus Christ our Savior.

Lent

Through Jesus Christ our Lord, who was tempted in every way as we are, yet did not sin. By his grace we are able to triumph over every evil, and to live no longer for ourselves alone, but for him who died for us and rose again.

or this

You bid your faithful people cleanse their hearts, and prepare with joy for the Paschal feast; that, fervent in prayer and in works of mercy, and renewed by your Word and Sacraments, they may come to the fullness of grace which you have prepared for those who love you.

Holy Week

Through Jesus Christ our Lord. For our sins he was lifted high upon the cross, that he might draw the whole world to himself; and, by his suffering and death, he became the source of eternal salvation for all who put their trust in him.

Easter

But chiefly are we bound to praise you for the glorious resurrection of your Son Jesus Christ our Lord; for he is the true Paschal Lamb, who was sacrificed for us, and has taken away the sin of the world. By Christ's death he has destroyed death, and by Christ's rising to life again he has won for us everlasting life.

Ascension

Through your dearly beloved Son Jesus Christ our Lord. After his glorious resurrection he openly appeared to the apostles, and in their sight ascended into heaven, to prepare a place for us; that where he is, there we might also be, and reign with him in glory.

Pentecost

Through Jesus Christ our Lord. In fulfillment of Christ's true promise, the Holy Spirit came down [on this day] from heaven, lighting upon the disciples, to teach them and to lead them into all truth; uniting peoples of many tongues in the confession of one faith, and giving to your Church the power to serve you as a royal priesthood, and to preach the Gospel to all nations.

Prefaces for Other Occasions

Trinity Sunday

For with your co-eternal Son and Holy Spirit, you are one God, one Lord, in Trinity of Persons and in Unity of Being; and we celebrate the one and equal glory of you, O Father, and of the Son, and of the Holy Spirit.

All Saints

For in the multitude of your saints, you have surrounded us with a great cloud of witnesses, that we might rejoice in their fellowship, and run with endurance the race that is set before us; and, together with them, receive the crown of glory that never fades away.

A Saint

For the wonderful grace and virtue declared in all your saints, who have been the chosen vessels of your grace, and the lights of the world in their generations.

or this

Because in the obedience of your saints you have given us an example of righteousness, and in their eternal joy a glorious pledge of the hope of our calling.

or this

Because you are greatly glorified in the assembly of your saints. All your creatures praise you, and your faithful servants bless you, confessing before the rulers of this world the great Name of your only begotten.

Apostles and Ordinations

Through the great shepherd of your flock, Jesus Christ our Lord; who after the resurrection sent forth the apostles to preach the Gospel and to teach all nations; and promised to be with them always, even to the end of the ages.

Dedication of a Church

Through Jesus Christ our great High Priest, in whom we are built up as living stones of a holy temple, that we might offer before you a sacrifice of praise and prayer which is holy and pleasing in your sight.

Baptism

Because in Jesus Christ our Lord you have received us as your beloved children, made us citizens of your kingdom, and given us the Holy Spirit to guide us into all truth.

Marriage

Because in the giving of two people to each other in faithful love you reveal the joy and abundant life you share with your Son Jesus Christ and the Holy Spirit.

Commemoration of the Dead

Through Jesus Christ our Lord; who rose victorious from the dead, and comforts us with the blessed hope of everlasting life. For to your faithful people, O Lord, life is changed, not ended; and when our mortal body lies in death, there is prepared for us a dwelling place eternal in the heavens.

Index

CPSIA information can be obtained
at www.ICGtesting.com
Printed in the USA
JSHW061241041222
34020JS00003B/3

9 781640 655621